Issues in Higher Learning Institutions

About the Author

Prof. Ganapathy Palanithurai, Rajiv Gandhi Chair for Panchayati Raj studies, Department of Political Science and Development Administration, Gandhigram Rural Institute–Deemed University, Gandhigram is an academic activist working with academic community, civil society, policy community and political community to impress upon them the importance and need of democratic local governance in India to enable the poor to lead a decent dignified human life. All his academic, research and outreach activities are being supported by an array of funding agencies namely the World Bank the UNDP, the UNICEF, the Hunger Project, SDC, DANIDA, Action Aid International, the Ford Foundation, Population Foundation of India, the Rajiv Gandhi Foundation, Toolkit Foundation, Netherland, Ministry of Panchayati Raj and State Planning commission. He was a visiting professor in Cologne University, Germany. He has to his credit seventy three books, 126 research articles, 112 popular articles in popular newspapers, 83 monographs published in a span of three decades. He is the coordinator of UGC-SAP and UGC innovative programmes. He held several administrative positions like Dean, Faculty of Social Sciences, Dean Student's Welfare, Member, Syndicate, Member Senate, Member, and Academic Council in Gandhigram Rural Institute. He was and is member of many advisory committees of the Government of India and Government of Tamil Nadu pertinent to local governance and rural development.

Issues in Higher Learning Institutions

G. Palanithurai

CONCEPT PUBLISHING COMPANY PVT. LTD.
NEW DELHI-110059

ISBN-13: 978-93-5125-300-6

First Published 2017

Published and Printed by

Concept
Since 1974

Concept Publishing Company Pvt. Ltd.
Regd. Office:
A/15-16, Commercial Block, Mohan Garden,
New Delhi-110059 (INDIA)
Phones : 25351460, 25351794, *Fax* : 091-11-25357109
E-mail : publishing@conceptpub.com
Website: www.conceptpub.com

Cataloging in Publication Data—DK Courtesy: D.K. Agencies (P) Ltd. <docinfo@dkagencies.com>

Palanithurai, G., author.
Issues in higher learning institutions / G. Palanithurai.
pages cm
Includes bibliographical references and index.
ISBN 9789351253006

1. Education, Higher—India. 2. Higher education and state—India. I. Title.

LA1153.P35 2017 DDC 378.54 23

TO
DIVINE MOTHER

Preface

Being an activist academic working in a rural institute for rural transformation hailing from a rustic rural family much concerned about the boys and girls coming from the rural areas mostly from the poor socio-economic background to the higher learning institutions with a hope that their socio-economic conditions would be transformed as education is a power instrument of change, go with disappointment from the higher learning institutions with certificates and degrees raised some fundamental questions about the academic transactions held in higher learning institutions. Basically, academic transactions are for the transformation of the communities and societies. But this is not taking place without getting transformation, students go with only certificates and diplomas. Students go out from the institutions only with disappointments. Their disappointment emanates from two aspects primarily they are going out not with the self-confidence that they can on their own to transform themselves and their families. Secondly, the certificates they acquire from the institutions do not carry any weight in the job market. Against this background, both students and their parents look at the social science programmes in the higher learning institutions in India today as non-utility courses. In reality as an active academic handling projects and visiting abroad as visiting professor mostly West, I found enormous opportunities for social science students. Opportunities are enormous not only in India, but also abroad. The students have to be informed that they can get enormous opportunities if they are equipped properly and go out from the institutions as professionals. They have to be prepared for a struggle. Students should be prepared for development struggle. The struggle should be joyful and meaningful. But it is not taking place in the educational institutions. I have sent a few students from our department to bilateral and multilateral agencies apart from sending them to some of the African countries under UNDP scheme. They do very well in those places and they make very good career. Those organizations are continuously asking for more number of students for social science research and teaching. In this context, I wanted to probe this problem of stagnation and non-seriousness. It is always my tendency to go in an unusual way to probe any issue. Basically, I rely on knowledge which is being brought forward by the stakeholders. Hence, I discussed those critical issues which plagued in the higher education system with the affected and their affiliates. Based on the responses given by the stakeholders, I have written articles in different periods and they have been published only through University News as it reaches the length and breadth of the country. It is done with an intention of evoking response from the academics. I got tremendous responses from academics from other universities which motivated me to bring all those articles in the form of a book. Twice I got letters from two leading publishing companies to compile the articles to publish them in the form of a book. Hence, this book is in the hands of the readers.

G. Palanithurai

Acknowledgements

In this book there are eleven chapters and all are articles published in "University News" in different periods. Academics who read my articles compelled me to elaborate certain articles and publish them in the form of a book. Subsequently, I continued to receive letters from two leading publishers to compile all the articles in the form of a monograph as all the themes are related to the process of education in higher learning institutions. Hence, I have done this work. First I must register my thanks to the editor and other responsible persons of University News for bringing out all my articles to a wide range of readers. Further, I should thank Mr. Ashok Kumar Mittal of the Concept Publishing Company (P) Ltd. and Mr. Garg of Gyan Books for having encouraged me to compile them in the form of a book. In fact while writing letters and speaking to me they have highlighted many of the aspects which I have written in those articles. In such a level they digested the stuff which I have given in the articles. Many of the colleagues in higher learning institutions used to criticize me for pointing out the lapses of the teachers and the institutions. Of course, there are many academics and vice-chancellors appreciated me for indicating the ills of the higher learning institutions. I consider that the criticisms and appreciations are the real motive factors to write more on this field. I always consider my work coming out from academic mill has got the efforts of many. Sometimes, the efforts are visible and mostly invisible. But, I firmly believe no work is the outcome of a single individual contribution. From conceptualization to publication many individuals role are involved. I first register my thanks to all those individuals who have given comments on the articles before publication. I register my thanks to my critiques after reading my articles. I also thank many for their appreciation and critical comments. Apart from the above, there are students who participated in my focus group discussions and one-to-one interaction brought several issues to me to write these articles. I sincerely express my thanks to them for having agreed to interact with me and stayed with me on this discourse. My colleagues of course are always a source of support. My twenty five years academic works in one place were enjoyable because of the support extended by my colleagues worked with me. Finally, my family unit is positive towards my academic works. I place on record my sincere thanks to my colleagues more specifically Prof. V. Ragupathy and my wife P. Mala. I also express my sincere thanks to all those individuals who directly and indirectly contributed to me for bringing out this book for the readers.

G. Palanithurai

Contents

List of Tables

List of Plates

1
Introduction

Higher education in India is in a critical juncture as it obviously facilitates a small section of the society to make wealth by leaving huge army as unemployed and unemployable despite its remarkable expansion in the past thirty years. No country in the world can match India in terms of its speed in expanding the higher learning institutions. Sudden expansion has its own advantages and disadvantages. Has the higher education system served the masses? Is the fundamental question to be probed. The market oriented economic activities transformed the higher education system as instruments to make money and wealth rather instruments of social change. No doubt the society gets transformed only through knowledge which is the product of higher education system. The question here is to whom it helps and works and who uses the knowledge? In this process, a new perception has been developed at present that education as instrument to earn profit. In this context, one has to note the fact the virtues and values nurtured through education over a period of time have sunk into oblivion. Educated aggressively involved in wealth making and profit making as they have invested huge amount of money in their education from preprimary to post-graduation. This thought process becomes a norm got the acceptance of the change making middle class. Once, education was considered as a powerful instrument to humanize the human society, but now it has turned the instrument to dehumanize the people. In such a way, education has been commodified as tradable and marketable commodity. The context makes everyone becomes an aspirant to enjoy material life. People develop aspiration to achieve material development. To achieve such material development education becomes a key. People invest money in education as they invest in business. People are being lured to invest money in education.

But in the marked era, there are different types of education. Education for rich, poor, marginalized, and middle class. People depending on their paying capacity, they decide the institutions. The problem we face today in higher education is the conditions of public institutions which are meant for poor. Because of the neoliberal policy, government has decided to allow the market forces to enter into education sector. As a result, the public institutions are marginalized, they are not being taken care of by the government. The education offered in the public institutions are poor in quality. These institutions are not led by real leaders with vision and determination. They are not in a position to steer the institutions. The leaders appointed by the authorities on political and other considerations have reduced the enthusiasm of the teachers. Completely, public institutions are demoralized, the institutional leaders neither have the needed capacity to manage change not mobilize adequate resources needed to the institutions. As a consequence of the above, the public institutions are starving for funds to meet the basic requirements of the institutions. The staff recruited for the public institutions are based not on merit due to political pressure. This syndrome has further weakened the public institutions. While making the public institutions weak, political authorities have adopted neoliberal policy and by which the public institutions are asked to compete in the market with other private institutions. The private institutions are led by CEO with adequate autonomy by adopting market principles whereas the public institutions are weakened by the political influence and bureaucratization.

Against this background, the public institutions have to function. Of the public institutions, there are institutions meant for elites and they grab all the opportunities of funding. These institutions are not serving the poor. Central universities, State universities, Public deemed universities and Government and aided colleges are facing the worst crises which they ever faced in Independent India.

In this context, what teachers in higher learning public institutions can do to overcome all those problems is a major question lingering in the minds of the conscious and concerned teachers. It is to be noted here that the teachers in the public institutions are the biggest beneficiaries in the new context. Their salaries are fatty and no pressure from above and below. Promotions are easy. Hence, majority keeps silence on many of the ills afflicting the higher education because their salaries are ensured. But a few teachers everywhere struggling to highlight the plight of the poor and the non-responsiveness of the policy community and administrative community to the needs of the poor. This group is a microscopic minority in any institution while is being not liked by the university administration. Yet relentlessly the struggle is going on. Being an academic activist and conscious teacher and a concerned citizen, I adopt an approach to sensitize teachers and managers of the university by doing action research and outreach programmes without accusing anybody. By doing so, I am making myself inevitable. But this strategy, I use to draw the attention of all. I use to write research articles in referred journals, popular articles for the public and policy community through newspapers both in English and Tamil. When I take up issues of education in higher learning institutions, I have a methodology of interacting with main stakeholders. Most of the interactions are face-to-face. Hence, I used to interact with students and teachers individually and collectively. I use to do, not only in our campus where I am working and I do it in different public institutions. Apart from the above, I interact with policy community and bureaucracy also. All those interactions are being brought out in the form of articles. They are being published in University News as it has been circulated length and breadth of the country. I have concentrated on some of the issues of higher education and brought out articles published through University News. After the publication of the articles, I received continuously letters from publishing houses and individuals to elaborate those articles and publish it as monographs. But I could not do it as I got several constraints. It could have done it if I got good quality researchers. Finding quality researchers in social science is very difficult at present.

It is my habit of preparing students hailing from rustic families for social science research. Once they equipped they go away for positions elsewhere. We cannot stop it. Yet we face the problem. Hence, we could not move fastly in academic ventures so fastly. Now, my friends compelled me to compile all those articles published in University News and put them in the form of a book. As a result, it has come out as a book.

Chapter on "Academic Freedom in Higher Learning Institutions: A Narrative from Personal Experience" explains the space available for teachers to work in teaching, research and outreach domains. It emphasises the role to be played by the academics to strengthen the institutions and help the students. I have drawn examples from the activities of the Department of Political Science and Development Administration, Gandhigram Rural Institute—Deemed University, Gandhigram. Effective and efficient teaching, doing socially relevant research and need-based outreach activities are in the domain of the teachers and for which Department unity, cohesiveness and research culture are the imperative needs. It all depends on the teachers unity for a larger cause. If that unity is achieved, tremendous activities can be carried out in all the domains without much financial outlay. The Department will have enormous energy and that will be released through all kinds of activities.

Chapter entitled "Accountability in Higher Learning Institutions" highlights the present conditions of accountability in higher learning institutions. The drive for accountability is always from the west. Any role to be performed either in family or in public institution, it is to be performed organically as '*Sudharma*'. Through internalization accountability is ensured in Indian Society. That was the culture practiced in India. The

Westernization and modernization have brought many practices to our institutions and organizations. They are being practiced mechanically and not organically. The problems we have been facing in higher learning institutions in establishing accountability are being discussed and what could be done at present are being explained in this chapter.

The Chapter "Interface between Academia and Policy Community" investigates the linkage between the academics and the policy-makers. The general assumption is that the academic institutions create knowledge and they are being used by the policy community to evolve suitable policies for solving problems and to achieve development. It is a truism that good policies, programmes and laws are the outcome of quality research that are coming out from the research institutions. In reality in India there is no connection between the two communities. Why this disconnect? Where from policy community gets knowledge? What is happening to the knowledge created in the academic institutions? Are they usable for policy-making? Are the questions raised and answered in this article. How to connect the academic communities with policy community has been highlighted based on the experience we had through our activities in the Department of Political Science and Development Administration, Gandhigram Rural Institute—Deemed University, Gandhigram.

Yet another chapter entitled "Non-Seriousness in Learning and Teaching in Social Science: A Micro-Analysis" critically investigates the issue of non-seriousness in studies among the Social Science students. This has been investigated by the author among the Social Science students in Gandhigram Rural Institute. It not only touched upon the non-seriousness of the students, it analysed the reason for why teachers are also non-serious in teaching research and outreach activities. The whole analysis is not to blame the students or teachers, but to find solution. Suggestions have been given as to how meaningful alternative Social Science programmes could be organized in higher learning institutions with the hope to raise seriousness among the students.

The chapter "Skill Development in Higher Learning Institutions: A Micro-Analysis" contextually investigates skill base of the students who are studying in social science branches of the institutions. It has assessed the challenges and barriers in the process of skilling the students. Remedies have been suggested to overcome the barriers and to make the students employable.

Of the functions of the higher learning institutions along with teaching and research, outreach is the key function and responsibility. Outreach activities have their own methodological nuances. They are to be carried out with the active participation of the students and teachers and for that purpose the students have to be trained and motivated through village placement programme. It is being organized by the Department of Political Science and Development Administration, Gandhigram Rural Institute, Deemed University, Gandhigram every year. The chapter entitled "Village Placement Programme: Learning about Communities" is a documentation of the experience gained by the students and teachers through the village placement programme held in an academic year. It is done by both teachers and students.

It is a quite interesting chapter titled "New Track for the New Vice-Chancellors", which brings to light the new roles and responsibilities the Vice-Chancellors have to perform contextually. Basically, universities are being led by mediocres and they are not able to show leadership and unable to contextualize the institutions. They become managers. As a result, universities are not enhancing the capacity and skill to face the new challenges coming from globalization and social transformation. This is the observation of many of the educationists and opinion-makers. The context requires new leaders to higher learning institutions to manage the change and the speed of the activities of the institutions. What are all the new responsibilities to be discharged and how they are to be discharged have been highlightened in the context of neo-liberalism in this chapter.

The chapter "Where We lead in Higher Education" brings out the critical issues which are affecting the higher education system and institutions. It touches on the growth path of the higher education in India and its related problems. Indian higher education has grown faster and as a result the higher education system has brought more of problems rather than strength to our economy or social transformative process. The quantum what we see in higher learning institutions in term of staff and students is an asset, but it does not look like an asset. It becomes a liability. To turn the liability into asset what could be done has been explained.

"New Paradigm of Social Science Research in the Era of Globalization" chapter brings to light the social and economic issues to be investigated in the new context of globalization. As we see the divide between the rich and the poor, the issues of the marginalized and neglected have to be focused. There are changes we have been noticing in development schemes, governance and administrative processes which require new perspective. Unless the academics understand the transformative process, meaningful research cannot be carried out in the institutions. In this chapter, major areas to be investigated and the major activities to be carried out in the community by the higher learning institutions have been listed.

"Quality Enhancement in Higher Learning Institution" is yet another chapter focusing its attention on the quality aspect of the products of the higher learning institutions. It is being looked at from the marketability of the students who are passing out from the higher learning institutions in the context of neo-liberalization. To ensure quality what are the steps to be taken, how they are to be taken, what institutional mechanisms are needed have been discussed in this chapter with a perspective.

Thus, some of the issues which are affecting the higher learning institutions have been investigated in the new context. The issues are being looked at from the point of view of Social Science.

2

Academic Freedom in Higher Learning Institutions

A Narrative from Personal Experience

Introduction

It is an axiomatic truth that higher learning institutions have a substantial role in shaping polity, society, policy and economy of any country in the world at present. Quality of activities in higher learning institutions decides the speed of socio-economic and political transformation of the societies. All the activities of higher learning institutions are around knowledge. Knowledge-based activities gain currency at present as new economy was borne, out of knowledge which is called 'knowledge economy'. Unequivocally, knowledge creation, knowledge updation, and knowledge dissemination are the main functions of the higher learning institutions. They contribute substantially for the transformation and well-being of human society through their three dimensional activities. The three dimensional activities of the higher learning institutions are research, academic (teaching) and extension (outreach) activities. All the activities of the higher learning institutions have to be carried out in the backdrop of a well defined policy formulated by the Government and the need articulated by the society. The higher learning institutions have to involve themselves in knowledge creation through their research and dissemination of the same through academic programmes. Further to disseminate knowledge, skill and information to the community directly, outreach programmes and schemes have to be chalked out. All the above activities have to be done with a sense of commitment to realize the basic objective of achieving human well-being.

All the activities of higher learning institutions have to directly or indirectly help the human collectivities to lead a decent and dignified human life. Hence, all the academic, research and outreach activities have to be constantly modified, and contextualised to suit the requirements of the society. They are to be done organically with a sense of dedication. Human society will find solutions to many of its problems in the process of education. Society gets substantial benefits from higher learning institutions. But this process has to happen in a free environment without much restrictions and barriers. While the teachers and students are on learning, both should enjoy freedom to make use of their full potentials. It is only through the process of education potentials of the human beings are brought out. There should not be any barrier or obstacle to those creative works. Thus, there will be a close link between the functioning of the Higher Learning Institutions and social, political and economic transformation of the society.[1] Academic institutions, academics and students should enjoy absolute freedom to pursue knowledge through the constant interaction between the teachers and the students from regulations of laws and interferences of any organization or state authorities or any social group. In Indian context how academic freedom works in higher learning institutions is being analysed through a case study from the perspective of teachers.

Context

Any issue for investigation has to be seen in the backdrop of the context apart from other factors which influences the issues. No doubt higher education is in the process of a dynamic transition leading to a volatile situation while responding to the challenges of globalization of economy.[2] To look at the higher learning institutions at present globalization of economy has to be kept in the backdrop. Because globalization has brought volley of changes in the society, polity and economy, its influence is huge in every aspect of the human society both negative and positive. In higher education also it brought changes. As economy expands in new dimensions, to keep up the momentum, it requires huge humanpower and they are to be produced only by the higher learning institutions. They are both skilled and knowledge labourers to meet the requirements in the labour market. The sudden expansion of higher learning institutions is inevitable. It is also true that sudden expansion will always cause damage to the quality of the product. Further, for the sudden expansion of the institutions huge investment is required and it is not available in the government. Hence, it is necessary to involve the private players in higher education sector. As a result, a sizeable number of institutions have been organized by the private agencies. They are in higher education sector to make profit by using the new opportunity of producing skilled and knowledge intensive labour force to meet the labour demands in India and abroad. Hence, the whole educational exercise has been driven towards labour market.

The main question here is to what extent the higher learning institutions have fulfilled the labour requirements in India and abroad through their academic programmes. While performing the above function to what extent the higher learning institutions have involved themselves in knowledge creation and knowledge updation through their research activities has to be analysed. Equally to what extent they are involved in outreach activities to connect themselves directly with the communities, has to be evaluated. To guide all the stakeholders who are in higher education several committees and commissions.[3] have been set-up and plethora of deliberative discourses had been conducted with the active involvement of knowledge leaders and institutional leaders.[4] In the process one would find conflicting and congruent perspectives on future of higher education in India which left the stakeholders in a fix.[5] From the trends in the functioning of decision-making bodies one could gauge where is our higher education and in which direction higher learning institutions are moving?[6]

In this context, a proper perspective should be in place for higher learning institutions. If one looks carefully, the functioning of higher learning institutions we can roughly presume that the institutions work for market[7] and thereby profits and employment became the guiding principles. Humanizing the human society, serving the society, working for human well-being, and social transformation have taken a backseat in the realm of higher education. Discourse, deliberation and debate in policy corridors are around growth, labour market, employment and profit. This tunnelled vision has hijacked the basic objective of education. Having seen the drift, hallow and shallow transformation in the outward activities of higher learning institutions, one can easily blame the policy-makers, state and market players. Where remedy lies is the basic question. Academics and researchers in the higher learning institutions are not the subordinates to carry-out the instructions from the above. They are thought leaders and creative individuals who are in all the bodies of the higher learning institutions and through their contributions in the respective bodies can bring needed changes in the functioning of institutions. Apart from influencing the decision-making process in the institutional set-up, they could bring changes in the institutions by discharging their responsibilities in a strategic way. Are the teaching communities in blame game or strategic player in changing the course of the institutions by their activities is the basic question? Now, the crucial role of academicians comes in the higher learning institutions. At least teachers should have freedom to develop perspective and based on the perspective academics can work for transformation of the human society from one level to another, through proper shaping of humanpower and do socially relevant research apart from conducting outreach programmes to reach out to the masses directly.

Conceptualization

Academic activities whether it is teaching or research or outreach, they are creative in nature. They are passionate development struggle and everyone should find joy in the process. They should be always innovative and transformative. Hence, these exercises have to be carried out without much barriers, obstacles, controls and bureaucratic regimes and regulations. They should be done in a conducive environment. It means freedom of teachers and students to teach, learn, pursue knowledge and research without interference from law, institutional regulations and public pressure. Teachers and students should have autonomy to pursue their programmes and bring out their observations, conclusions based on their research pursuits.[8] The justification for academic freedom lies not in the convenience of the teachers, but in the utility of opportunities and facilities for the betterment of the society. Ultimately, the whole exercise is revolved around seeking truth. Never society accepts truth the moment it is revealed through research from the days of societies. It has to cross through processes of barriers and obstacles. Truth has reached the society only through a prolonged struggle.

Academic freedom became an important subject of debate because academic community faces plethora of obstacles while pursuing research to seek truth. Academic freedom refers to pursuit of academic programme, research and outreach activities by the teachers and students in a free environment without much barriers and they should not face any restriction because of state laws, or regulation of institutions or pressure from any social groups. Academics have to design academic programmes, research projects and outreach activities without the restriction of the Government and its institutions. It had been witnesses in eighteenth and nineteenth century that the newly emerged nation states of Europe had imposed regulations to the universities that they have to function as per the direction of the state. The teachers have to teach what the Governments have approved for teaching. Government can facilitate, coordinate and supervise the academic institutions to check whether these institutions create everlasting impact in the society. It is not only the restrictions on academic, research and outreach activities or programmes of the teachers in higher learning institutions, but also on the methodology adopted by the teachers to carry out on those programmes.

While academic freedom is being considered as basic requirement for the academician to create knowledge, it is to be underlined that freedom goes with responsibility. In every action related to academic programme, research and extension activities, the teacher concerned should have more responsibilities, concerns and self-restraints. Teachers are not onlookers or spectators to watch what is going on in the society, polity and economy. They are active players, partners and participants. How they play their roles and discharge the responsibilities determine the course of the functioning of the institutions. Through their functioning in the higher learning institutions, they can turn the whole process of social transformation.[9]

A teacher in higher learning institution has three major responsibilities. They are teaching, research and outreach activities and in all the three aspects he or she can do innovation and bring changes contextually which ultimately benefit the larger communities apart from student community.[10] All the activities are highly dynamic and fast as they are technologically driven and linked with global transformation. All their actions should be in the backdrop of the transformations that takes place in the region, nation and the world. Hence, all the local actions have to be designed and carried out in the context of global changes and transformations. Contextual updation of academic programmes, doing research on socially relevant issues and connecting the learning institutions with the communities by providing ideas, information, knowledge and skill relating to the development of the stakeholders are the imperative activities on the part of the teachers in higher learning institutions which require an environment in the institutions which are to be provided by the institutional authorities.[11] It is to be noted here that institutional environment is the creation not only by the involvement of authorities, but also with the active participation of the teachers and the students. All the activities have to happen in a cultural setting. That culture has to be created in the institutions mostly with the involvement of the teachers and active participation of the learners or students. The question here is to what extent the institutions have created such an environment and to what extent the teachers have utilized the environment to discharge the roles and responsibilities. More specifically to what extent the teachers are conscious in shaping a culture in the higher learning institutions for free flow of thought and social transformation.

In India, higher learning institutions have governance regulations as per the regulations of the UGC and the Central Government. Mostly those regulations are relating to administering the institutions. Even the governance structure provides opportunity for the academics to be in governance structure to decide the academic matters. Academic matters are being decided only in academic council and Board of Studies wherein senior teachers serve as members. For academic excellence, those bodies never cause any damage if the academics prepare well for the academic programmes. Enjoying academic freedom depends on how teachers use those opportunities by designing an academic programme, doing research on socially relevant theme, and carryout outreach programmes to communities. Academic programmes can be designed suitable to the requirements of the community. It should be need-based and socially relevant. The programme can be started with a focus to meet the societal needs. Equally the research and outreach activities have to be linked with the community needs. How academics work in a higher learning institution in what environment is explained through a case study in this chapter. It is a narrative of the academic, research and extension activities of a Department of an University.

The basic assumption for this analytical narration is that the teachers have enormous freedom to chalk out academic research and outreach programmes and if they exercise the freedom conferred on them, at least public institutions will prepare sensible, sensitive qualified skilled and knowledge persons for social transformation. If a teacher is conscious, whether the institution has got perspective or not he/she can develop a perspective and with the perspective he or she can discharge all the responsibilities in meaningful way to bring expected social transformation. With this assumption, the present chapter explains how a Department is able to demonstrate its potential to draw the attention of the policy-makers, donor agencies, government departments and foreign agencies through its committed academic, research and outreach actions.

Case Analysis

It is a story about the activities of a small Department (the Department of Political Science and Development Administration, the Gandhigram Rural Institute – Deemed University) in a centrally funded Deemed University since 1991.[12] Author of this chapter joined the Department of Political Science and Development Administration in 1991. It was a small Department with three teaching faculty members including the author. A small room was provided to all the three and beyond that there was no other facility. The Department had only a bachelor degree on 'Development Administration'. The author was given the responsibility of heading the Department. Two of his colleagues did not have Ph.D. in 1991. The nomenclature of the degree was B.DA (Bachelor of Development Administration) which was not in the degree list approved by the UGC. In this context, the Department wanted to change the academic programme totally to suit the requirements of the society and to bring the programme under the framework of the UGC and to suit the requirement of the market. While doing so, a perspective was kept in the backdrop. Essentially, the perspective is Gandhian framework of development. Hence, in consultation with other colleagues, the Department has introduced a new five year integrated masters' programme on "Development Administration" in 1996-97. During that period the integrated programme was new. The main objective of the programme is to prepare middle level managers for development orgainzations. It was a felt need for many of the development organizations which implement development schemes and programmes professionally and they could not get the adequate number of professionals fully trained in the field. The syllabus for the innovative programme was prepared in an unusual way by inviting representatives from civil society, research institutions, civil service and academics to Board of Studies. It was an interdisciplinary programme with an emphasis on practice. To prepare a marketable product to the labour market through this programme market needs have been packaged in the programme. When the whole proposal and programme were placed in the Academic Council, almost all the members opposed it by bringing an argument that students will find it difficult to get scholarship, they cannot write public service commission examinations and cannot get recognition as there is no corresponding subject in social science in other universities. Because during that period no university in India was offering either undergraduate or post-graduate programme in Development Administration. Universities both Central and State offered only post-graduate programme in public administration. Development administration was only a paper offered in Public administration programme. An appeal was made in the academic council that it is an experiment and the Department is taking risk and responsibility and hence the resolution may be passed. Convincingly the author as Head of the Department has explained the members that the programme came in the present shape after a prolonged discourses, deliberations and discussions with different strata of stakeholders. The council has taken two hours to deliberate this proposal. With much difficulty, the Department has got the approval from the Academic Council. The university has got the approval from the UGC and Government of Tamil Nadu. It is equated with M.A. Public Administration by the Government of Tamil Nadu. Students of the Department who have undergone this programme have got opportunity to clear JRF, NET and many went to public service. A few became faculty members in Central universities and universities in Ethiopia. Till date it is going on well. Having seen the success of the programme many of the departments have been asked to make such a venture to introduce five year integrated programme by the authorities.

But nobody was ready to take such a risk as the Department of Political Science has faced many barriers in getting scholarship, and recognition from the Government of Tamil Nadu. The Department of Political Science and Development Administration of the Gandhigram Rural Institute has got 109 M.A. students, 7 M.Phil. and 18 Research Scholars are on the roll. It is one of the leading centres in specializing on 'decentralization'. The Department had taken a conscious decision to specialize on decentralized governance and decentralized development in the year 1991.

In the university system, nobody has instructed the Department to introduce five year integrated programme and to specialize in 'decentralization'. It was the conscious decision of the faculty members. The Department only initiated all the proposals. In order to increase rigour in the programme, the Department took initiative to appoint Adjunct Professors from the field of practice. Retired civil servants Mr. S.S. Meenakshisundaram, Mr. T.R. Ragunandan and S. Swaminathan, have been invited to serve the Department as Adjunct Professors. The Board of Management of the university has approved it. To sensitize the students on some of the sensitive subjects, the Department has involved some of the Development organizations to conduct training programmes. They conduct training programmes to the students regularly. While strengthening the academic programme initiative was taken to create Rajiv Gandhi Chair for Panchayati Raj Studies. This chair was created only for a specific purpose of strengthening research and outreach programmes. This was the first Rajiv Gandhi Chair created in India not with the resources given by the UGC. It was our creation supported by many agencies. Through the chair series of research projects have been undertaken. Equally capacity building for local body leaders has been conducted by the chair. It became a resource agency for the institutions which are involved in strengthening local body institutions. It started doing policy advocacy for strengthening local body institutions based on the reports prepared by the chair. Having seen the works of the chair, four Members of Parliament have contributed ten lakh rupees each from their MPLAD fund for constructing a separate building for the activities of the chair. The chair has drawn the attention of many donor agencies. The Hunger Project, Population Foundation of India, the Ford Foundation, the UNDP, the World Bank, DANIDA, the State Planning Commission, UNICEF, Ministry of Panchayati Raj, Government of India, and Toolkit Foundation, Netherland have supported financially the action research of the Rajiv Gandhi Chair. It brought out series of publications for the benefit of local body leaders, researchers and academics who are specializing in local governance. It reframed the syllabus of a paper on 'Local Governance' for both undergraduate and post-graduate students of social science discipline in the universities of Tamil Nadu. It conducted series of workshops for the staff reporters of Newspapers and electronic media on the importance of new local governance. The Rajiv Gandhi Chair has brought out a news supplement for local bodies through a vernacular newspaper for one year by signing a MoU with the management of the newspaper '*Dinamalar*'. It was one full page newspaper supplement entitled "*Panchayat Malar*" on every Monday. Subsequently radio broadcasting was done through All India Radio Chennai throughout Tamil Nadu for local bodies entitled "Good Governance through Local Governance". The programme was prepared by the Rajiv Gandhi Chair and sponsored by the Hunger Project and broadcasted every Monday between 7.00 to 7.30 evening. It went on for about six months. On request by many stakeholders, a website has been exclusively created for Rajiv Gandhi Chair (www.rajivgandhichairgri.com). Based on the rich experience in local governance, the Department applied for SAP in UGC and the Department has been sanctioned the programme for five years and subsequently also it was approved by the UGC. The Department has also offered an innovative M.A. programme on 'Governance and Development' sanctioned by the UGC. In the Department only six faculty members are involved in teaching, research and extension activities. Having seen the activities of the Department, Centre for Modern Indian Studies, Cologne University, Germany has invited a professor from the

Department as visiting professor to teach governance and society in India to the masters students for a semester. Based on the visits to Germany by our professor, two MoU have been signed between Hannover and Cologne universities in Germany and the Gandhigram Rural Institute for exchange of students and researchers. Based on the MoU students and research scholars are coming for internship and research in India. Researchers from the Gandhigram Rural Institute have gone to Cologne University. It enabled the periodical visits of Cologne and Hannover universities professors to India and our institute professors to universities in Germany. In such a way, the Department has worked hard to draw the attention of the Central and State Governments and local bodies. It has drawn the attention of donor agencies both bilateral and multilateral. Through its actions, the institute has got visibility. The Department has been fully equipped infrastructurally through the projects. Through its actions the Department has

Box 2.1: Global to Local

The Rajiv Gandhi Chair for Panchayati Raj studies had taken initiative to federate the elected women representatives of rural local bodies in Tamil Nadu with the support of the Ford Foundation. It was successfully done by registering it as an independent body. It was well appreciated by the Ministry of Panchayati Raj and it was subsequently followed in other states with the support of various funding agencies. The whole process was well documented and published. Having seen the work of the chair, a challenging question was posited to us. It is nothing, but looking at globalization from the perspective of decentralization. This initiative was also supported by the Ford Foundation. The chair has conducted series of studies in Tamil Nadu on the life and livelihood of the poor. The primary objective of the study is to analyze the opportunities and threats of globalization of economy. The study has identified the opportunities and threats. Further the chair has found out strategies to make use of the opportunities for the benefit of the poor and to avoid threats by using decentralization. Based on the findings, a training module has been prepared and by using the training module Gram Panchayat leaders have been trained to manage globalization. In order to disseminate the findings of the study on globalization and decentralization a newsletter was published periodically entitled "Global to Local" and circulated among the Panchayats and civil society organizations. Series of monographs and working papers have been written based on the data collected for the project. By doing this action research, the chair has demonstrated the concern and commitment of the faculty towards the poor and the marginalized. Relevance and action is the key of the Rajiv Gandhi Chair for Panchayati Raj studies.[13]

demonstrated that it is an inevitable Department. Among the Departments in Social Science, Rural Development and Humanities, the Department of Political Science and Development Administration is only the SAP department in the institute. By seeing the activities eight donor agencies have created endowments in the Department. Annually, endowment lectures have been arranged by inviting intellectuals and practitioners who are working in the critical issues of development of marginalized groups. All these activities were possible only through a process of crossing barriers and obstacles. The university authorities have always been positive and supportive towards all the activities of the Department despite academic politics. It is learnt from this struggle that

Box 2.2: Making the Panchayats to Respond to Natural Disaster

When Tsunami struck the Coastal areas of Tamil Nadu, the Rajiv Gandhi Chair involved itself in relief, rehabilitation and reconstruction in 17 Gram Panchayats in Nagapattinam District with the support of Swiss Development Cooperation, New Delhi. In all the 17 Gram Panchayats the chair has facilitated the Gram Panchayats to prepare a reconstruction plan with the active participation of the people with the support of the Hunger Project. These activities have been carried out in a period of five years. Further, the role of Panchayats in Disaster Preparedness was studied in three states (Andhra Pradesh, Orissa and Tamil Nadu) and based on the study report a training module was prepared. Subsequently, a training programme was organised for the Gram Panchayat presidents from the coastal areas with the support of Action Aid International. Nearly 400 Gram Panchayat leaders have been trained on disaster preparedness and disaster management. Several reports have been prepared out of this project for policy advocacy.[14]

Box 2.3: Transformative Leadership

Electing a leader is in the hands of the people, but shaping the elected representative as a transformative leader is in the hands of the higher learning institutions. The above is the proposition of the Rajiv Gandhi Chair. Hence, it evolved a training module to conduct leadership training programme for the elected representatives with the support of the Hunger Project and the Rajiv Gandhi Foundation. Nearly 8000 Gram Panchayat leaders have been trained. Of them majority are women and *Dalit* leaders. After the training, several refresher programmes have been conducted. Three years after conducting the training programme assessment studies have been conducted and the reports have been published. It is about the impact of the training programme. Major achievements of the leaders have been documented through a new case study method and the same document was also published.[15]

the academics can enjoy freedom only through committed action for larger benefits of the community and society.

Box 2.4: Village Placement Programme

Every year a seven day village placement is being organized for the students and by which teachers and students have to stay in a village and work with the people for the benefit of students and the community. Teachers will also get benefits out of this programme. Last year the author coordinated the programme. Students have been placed in a village Panchayat area where 80 per cent of the people are *Dalit* families. In the seven days stay the students have interacted with the community to find out the reason for the backwardness of the area and the people. The whole process was documented and published as a small monograph and in which what the community and the students have benefited have been explained in detail.[16]

Box 2.5: Working with Civil Society Organization

'Evidence' is a resource agency functioning at Madurai, Tamil Nadu on social justice issues. Periodically, it conducts research for policy advocacy. The Rajiv Gandhi chair use to work with Evidence for strengthening the local bodies in addressing the issues of the *Dalits*. Evidence conducts periodical survey research to assess the conditions of the poor *Dalits* in Tamil Nadu. It organises public hearing for policy advocacy. Once that task is over, it does not make use of the data. Since the chair closely work with the agency for its advocacy work we made use of the data to prepare articles and monographs for larger consumption of the researchers those who are working on social justice and governance issues.[17]

Conclusion

It is a considered opinion that teachers are enjoying utmost freedom in Indian higher education for their three dimensional activities provided they made themselves inevitable in terms of their academic achievements. Though universities are not free from politics, and bureaucratic web, academics can make a difference by their academic performance and thereby they can make the university authorities to listen to them. The question here is, have our academics taken such a course in their academic activities in the university system. Opportunities are sky high if one explores the domain and area for specialization as India provides varieties of issues for investigation. In globalization that opportunity has been expanded to the global level. To make use of the opportunities, the academics have to equip themselves in building their capacity, skill and capability. For social science academics today tremendous opportunities are waiting as donor agencies are liberally funding individual and group projects to carry out research on socially relevant areas or on the problems affecting the social life. Yet another area outreach programme is virgin field. If one takes up extension activities in the subject on which he or she specializes, immense opportunity for getting social recognition. UGC need not give grants for equipping our departments infrastructurally, but by carrying out funded projects from bilateral and multilateral agencies apart from UGC, ICSSR and the ministries, huge funds can be mobilized. From the funds, the whole department can be equipped. Instead of looking for funds from the university authorities academics can generate funds for equipping themselves and to equip the Department. Faculty members have to learn for waging development struggle. By nurturing a leadership to make others to join in the development struggle, teachers in the higher learning institutions have to consciously enhance their capacity to perform their responsibilities such as teaching, research and outreach activities, professionally.

Notes and References

1. Palanithurai, G., (2012), *Social Relevance of Higher Learning Institutions*, New Delhi: Concept Publishing Company Pvt. Ltd.
2. Palanithurai, G., (2010), "Higher Education in India: Where are We Leading", *University News*, Vol. 48: No. 28, July 12-18.
3. Agarwal, Pawan (2007), "From Kothari Commission to Pitroda Commission", *Economic and Political Weekly*, 17th February.
4. University Grant Commission (2007), "A Brief Report of the National Conference on Development of Higher Education", New Delhi: University Grant Commission.
5. Joseph Thomas, (2007), "Commission *versus* Commission in Higher Education", *Economic and Political Weekly*, December 15.
6. Panikkar, K.N. (2009), "Towards a New Paradigms in Education", *The Hindu*, 9th May.
7. Ministry of Human Resource Development (2009), *"Report of the Committee to Advice on Renovation and Rejuvenation of Higher Education"*, New Delhi: Government of India.

8. Rajkumar, C., (2007), "Academic Freedom and Higher Education", *The Hindu,* 13th November.
9. National Knowledge Commission (2009), *Report to the Nation 2006,* New Delhi: National Knowledge Commission.
10. Palanithurai, G., (2009), "Larger Role of Academics in Rural Human Life", *University News",* Vol. 47, No. 16, April.
11. Palanithurai, G., (2012), "New Task for the New Vice-Chancellors", *University News,* Vol. 50, No. 21, May 21-27.
12. Rajiv Gandhi Chair, (2007), *Ten Years of Experience in Decentralization,* Gandhigram: Rajiv Gandhi Chair for Panchayati Raj Studies.
13. Palanithurai, G., (2012), *Globalization and Rural Development,* New Delhi: Concept Publishing Company Pvt. Ltd., Palanithurai, G. (2007), *Globalization and Decentralization,* New Delhi: Concept Publishing Company Pvt. Ltd.
14. Palanithurai, G., (2007), *Panchayats in Disaster Preparedness and Management,* New Delhi: Concept Publishing Company Pvt. Ltd.
15. Palanithurai, G., (2002), *Capacity Building Exercises for Local Body Leaders,* New Delhi: Concept Publishing Company Pvt. Ltd.
16. Palanithurai, G., (2014), *Village Placement Programme: An Experiment in Learning,* New Delhi: Concept Publishing Company Pvt. Ltd.
17. Palanithurai, G., (2013), *Status of Dalits and Dalit Representatives in Rural Local Bodies,* New Delhi: Concept Publishing Company Pvt. Ltd.

3
Accountability in Higher Learning Institutions

Introduction

At present accountability, transparency, and good governance are the most debated concepts both in public and academic fora. Modicum of literature has been produced on the above subjects by the scholars based on the experience in the world. The very purpose of such discourses on the subjects is not to produce debatable reports, books and articles, but to prepare actionable guides to change the mode of governance and administration with a view to serve the people better as the system of governance and administration established in the world has not delivered the goods to the level of the expectation of the masses. After the advent of globalization, the above process has been intensified with a view to make the functioning of institutions and organizations more effective and efficient in delivering goods and services. Many of the countries in the world are pursuing this course vigorously with an objective of achieving better results in delivery of services. Of course, there are visible actions in this regard from village Panchayat to federal government at present in our country. But the moot question here is to what extent people at the receiving end have benefitted out of the new strategic devices for ensuring accountability in governance and administration. To demonstrate the current phase of the ensuring accountability process, an attempt is made in this chapter to analyse the accountability in higher learning institutions in India.

Setting

Accountability, academic audit, performance evaluation, accreditation and quality certification are the new concepts slowly picking up in higher learning institutions in India. They are in active deliberation and discourses in the authoritative bodies of the higher learning institutions and regulatory and grant giving bodies of our country. Slowly institutional structures have been created in this regard to put into practice all the new concepts. But it does not mean that this new process has been accepted by all in higher learning institutions. Considerable number of academics have expressed their reservation over the establishment of these new institutional mechanisms and processes for ensuring accountability. Yet initiatives are on in the higher learning institutions to move further in this regard as per the direction of the funding agencies with the support of a large number of academics as the supporting academics are conscious and sensitive on the changes that are taking place in the world.[1] The globalization of economy has removed the barriers for knowledge workers to cross the borders of countries and continent for gaining employment opportunities. This kind of migration of knowledge workers needs standardization of questions.[2] The whole transformation is driven by the economic globalization.[3] People those who can get advantage out of this accreditation and standardization support the new initiatives and others oppose as they are not the beneficiaries of the new initiatives. Yet this issue should not be looked at from the perspective of beneficiaries and non-beneficiaries. One has to look at this issue beyond the narrow consideration. Logically, one has to look at this new initiative from the perspectives of main stakeholders students whether they get any substantial benefit out of this exercise.

As a result it becomes a contested issue and subject in the higher learning institutions academic agenda. People who oppose this new initiative and mechanism bring an argument that academic institutions and academics should enjoy autonomy and freedom and this new dispensation is interfering in the autonomy of the institutions and academics. But this kind of opposition and arguments are with a basic idea of resisting change and subject themselves for scrutiny. People who support this new initiative bring an argument that it brings quality enhancement in research and academic activities and it makes the products from the academic institutions more suitable to job market in the new context. To ensure accountability this is the best instrument and process. The new initiative is a drive and it makes the people who are all involved in the job to achieve a target with a focus. Target achievement always drives the system and the system operators. Further the whole analysis moves from output to outcome. Apart from the above there is yet another argument that the accountability policy, decision and discourses are on paper only and the ground reality is that there is no trace of accountability at the ground. Everything goes as usual, but at the time of assessment and evaluation, the stakeholders prepare reports and they are also prepared by themselves as self-assessment reports. Report preparation becomes a nuanced activity rather than the main activities of the stakeholders. So, there is a disconnect between policy and practice. Against this background, accountability in higher learning institutions in India is being investigated.

Background

The new mechanism for accountability in higher learning institutions what we wanted to evolve and practice in India had been in the US long back well before Europe has adopted. The US is the pioneer in establishing this accountability culture in the world. The US had achieved what it wanted to achieve through the institutional mechanism and practices established. The results the US has achieved through this process made other countries to follow. Europe has also followed the same from the practice of the US.[4] The new initiatives and practices have yielded good results in achieving economic growth and development in the US and the European countries. Having seen the positive results of the new mechanisms and practices, many countries in the world wanted to adopt these initiatives with an objective of getting advantage out of globalization by producing high quality human power for world labour market. It was considered as a best tool to solve the problem of unemployment in their countries by enhancing the quality of education suitable to the market needs. The ultimate end is to infuse quality and relevance in education. In this context one has to understand the concept of education has been directly linked to profit making and gaining economic advantage. The old principles of education namely preparing human being for higher level activities for human evolution has been given a goby. While tracing the origin of this thinking one can easily locate the whole exercise has been taken from business, trade and industry.[5] It brought a simple equation of investment and return. To the investment made thereof in a venture what profit we get is the question linked to higher education also. Since, huge money came from the business to higher education for research and academic programmes, the question of profit emerges as a key factor in the whole process. How quality took centre stage in the process of education is yet another question. This is due to expectation generated from education to make profit. Education process involves a huge investment at present. The basic economic argument, investment and profit which made the system conscious of its functioning and performance in the north and the west. As a result they have achieved tremendous results both in output and outcome. Large number of outcome measures have been developed for the academic and research programmes only after the introduction of the new accountability system in higher learning institutions. To ensure quality an array of steps, instruments and strategies have been evolved and practiced. The whole exercise yielded results which have contributed for the economic development of the country and the society. Hence, it prompted others to follow. It is to be noted here that wherever the innovations have been done in the West, they were all conscious efforts with a sense of commitment and sincerity, whereas the places where the practices and processes are borrowed and adopted based on the West have brought mixed responses. Mostly they become symbols and rituals. Even in Europe, the practice was not fully endorsed by the teachers. In Europe, this issue has been critically analysed. Yet they have agreed to the logic of introducing such a kind of devices to improve the quality of education. No one has disputed over the argument that quality of education has to be enhanced with a purpose of increasing the employability of the students coming out from the academic institutions with certificates.

Indian Practice

In India now it has been a practice to place certain procedures and processes for ensuring accountability. Self-evaluation report, student evaluation of teachers, institutional accreditation by NAAC, submitting institutional profile for seeking funds for activities, and academic audit are some of the exercises in this regard. Despite the above the quality of education has not improved and as a result we find more graduates coming out from the educational institutions unemployable as their skill and capacity are not to the expected standard of the market.[6] Our quantitative growth of education has not brought out any significant change in the labour market. Hence, a natural question arises as to what extent accountability is ensured to the stakeholders. If the accountability is ensured why then the quality is not enhanced.

It is imperative to precisely explain the concept 'accountability'. Accountability is answerability. For any action someone is responsible and the person who is performing the job is accountable to the people for whom the job is being performed. It is an obligation to report and respond to the people who get benefit out of any act or job. Who is responsible to whom and for what and how? is the basis of accountability. Basically, it is an exercise to keep the institutions, organizations groups and individuals responsible for the resources spent. It is an exercise to find out when resources are spent whether the money spent has produced the expected results. This exercise has to be done through a process with some institutional mechanisms. To ensure accountability, there are institutional mechanisms and they work through tools. In higher education system, the above devices have been introduced to bring accountability that too in a context. The context is massification of education and expansion of education by involving the private in an unfathomable measure. It is a larger debate whether the private players can be allowed in the education section as the state does not have adequate resources to expand the higher education massively to meet the market needs. By quoting the examples from the west arguments have been projected that private will play a meaningful role when state regulate them properly and enable them fastly. From the past two decades experiences one can not say that private has played havoc and equally one cannot say all private have added strength and contributed postiviely. The entry of private players in education has increased the enrollment rate. Because of the entry of the private, the government wants to regulate them by putting the regulatory mechanism. At the same time, the private has got a perspective that it has to be in a business mode. Unless the quality is enhanced, the products saleability will be at risk. There are private institutions in the new context which invests heavily and concentrate on the educational processes seriously and consciously and they draw the attention of the world. Equally another set of institutions have entered into the domain of education with a keen interests in making high profit by making use of the new opportunities. They are non-serious players yet they are also on the job. Apart from the above public institutions have been started both by the Central and State governments. Even among the public institutions there are two categories of institutions as we found in private.[7] In order to enhance quality and bring standard, the accountability mechanism is envisaged. The processes envisaged and tools devised for such accountability mechanism are more or less the same as we find in the West and north. In the north the tools and mechanisms were consciously evolved with the determination to achieve the impact in the society. It was just like a business plan. Having seen the results in the North America, Western European Government wanted to emulate the same as they also wanted to achieve results in economy and society. Yet there are reservations. Whereas in India, it has been resolved to go for establishing accountability mechanism to enhance the quality and bring standard in the educational programme to meet the new demands emerged out of globalization for workforce not only in India but also the other countries in the world. No doubt, the objectives, aims and goals are lofty, but the process of implementation is tardy and weak. It is a well-known fact that the evaluation has more of quantitative aspects and qualitative aspects which can be generated by the teachers to the level of expectation while evaluating the institutions. The evaluation practices become rituals rather than a culture. It has helped the teachers to build their career rather than contributing to the shaping of good quality products from the educational institutions to the labour market.

Though the higher education sector in India has accepted the new target without resistance it has facilitated in the process of implementation. As a result accountability in education is implemented in form and not in content and substance. No doubt it has achieved some instrumental value but not intrinsic value. Reasons for this state of affairs are manyfold. It can be traced from federal decision-making to students perception and perspective of learning. Instead of the quality enhancement, quality deterioration takes place in the education sector and youth are lured and deceived collectively. It is obvious from the swelling army of educated unemployables in the country while the industrial service and agricultural and social sectors are in need of more professionals.[8] The pronounced objective in the context is achieving demographic dividend, but the ground actions are not conscious and professional. It is the reality and what is to be done in this regard is the moot question everyone has to ponder over. There is no dispute over the basic objective of bringing accountability in the educational institution. How it is to be ensured and thereby the expected quality can be achieved and thereby economic growth and social development can be achieved?

To give answer I take the base argument of my students in a classroom. After a brief discussion about the concept accountability in the class a student asked me a question who is answerable to whom? Who is accountable to whom? How accountability system is built in the governance and administrative institutions? In the hierarchical governance architecture upward accountability is legally built. Really the system has to serve the masters. People are the real masters. But they are not legally empowered to make the government servants to ensure accountability. Government dominants and the institutions created are answerable to themselves hierarchically. From the lowest unit of governance and administration to highest unit accountability is built upward. Hence, the servants have to answer and accountable to their legal masters namely their supervisors. In the same way, the teachers in the educational institutions are accountable morally to the students but legally they are answerable to the system which has created accountability built in can be ensured and quality can be achieved. Against the background one has to ask a question. Is there any scope in the system to make the teachers answerable to the students? Students are coming to higher learning institutions with hope and aspirations. To meet the hopes and aspirations of the students, teachers have to work. Preparing them for the job market is the main job now for the teachers. Are the teachers conscious of their role and responsibility contextually. Students are made accountable to the teachers and not *vice versa*. Students are at the receiving end. Is there any possibility for the teachers to get reward when they prepare the students with potential to get employment opportunity? Neither there is no incentive nor disincentive for the teachers for their best and worst performance respectively. From syllabus preparation to answer script evaluation students have to have space for questioning. The above questions have been raised by the students. I have asked them to find out solution to establish the accountability mechanism. They suggested that the accountability mechanism which is in vogue has to be reversed and it should be made downward accountability mechanism where beneficiaries have to play a major role in bringing accountability on the part of the system.

How to bring the students in the system as principal participants is the question. Since, I had a Western experience I have shared with my students some of my experiences in the Western countries. When I was serving as Guest Professor in Cologne University, Germany, I was brief about the nuances to be adopted while conducting classes in Cologne University. Class-room is the space for both teachers and students. I have offered three courses during the semester. During that period I have followed certain practices. First practice what adopted is whenever I apply leave I have to inform the students first and later only I inform the chairperson of the Department. While informing them I have to suggest works to be carried out by the students during that allotted hour. Secondly, the classroom teaching was not a delivery of lecture alone. It was a discussion and discourse and the students have participated effectively as prior briefing was done as what we are going to discuss in the next class. Moreover, reference materials have been suggested to them. For all my classroom activities I was ably assisted by a teaching assistant at the level of Assistant Professor. As a result, the students come prepared to participate in the classroom discussion. The total discussion in the classroom was recorded and it was prepared as a report. The report was to be prepared only by the students and the report has to be corrected by the teacher. For each class one student has to do that exercise. Thus, everyone in the group has got an opportunity to record the classroom discussion. After the class hour is over, he or she on the same day sit with other students collect details from other students also and prepare the report. The teachers receive the report on the next day. The teacher has to go through the report and correct the same. The teaching assistant has to help the teacher to correct the report. Once the corrections are carried out, the report is being sent to the students through a group Email. ID. Once the semester is over every student will have a report on the classroom discussion. It comes to near about a Ph.D. thesis. Thus, it was a rigorous work for the students and the teacher. Both have to work and it was a learning exercise and not teaching. Both are engaged tightly and joyfully and in the process both are in the learning process. Further, worksheet has to be prepared by the teacher and they are to be worked by the students. Once the worksheet exercise was done by the students, they are to be evaluated by the teachers. While distributing the corrected worksheets, the teachers have to give reply to the queries of the students. Thus, teachers are in the hands of the students. In the whole process, both students and the teachers are becoming serious and conscious of their jobs and assignments. Both are tightly engaged, need-based engagement and joyful engagement. In such a way learning has been programmed and designed. From the syllabus preparation to worksheet evaluation students role is crucial and for which both have to be conscious and committed. In the whole process teacher has been involved in such a way that he or she is in the hands of the students.

The above aspects which I have narrated from my experience in Germany to the students, and the worksheet prepared by me and exercised by the students shown to them have created a sense that not only the teachers but also the students have to work hard and struggle. Then only the students have to be real challenges to the teachers and thereby the teachers can be engaged tightly and they can be made answerable to the stakeholders. This is the downward accountability system. The present day accountability system of doing academic audit, self-evaluation report, performance assessment report, and accreditation are nothing, but *quid pro guo* system. Teacher's reports are being evaluated by teachers. Teachers have been trained to prepare self-assessment report and formats have been devised by the institutions. One set of teachers recognize the services of another set of teachers in the name of peer review. Large number of teachers are involved in this exercise and it becomes a credit for the teachers. Huge money is being spent on this kind of peer review exercise meant for establishing accountability. It becomes a ritual rather than a culture. It becomes a mechanical exercise rather than organic learning practices. It has created only careerism rather than a quality culture. Indian higher learning institutions have evinced interest in following the Western model of accountability in form and not in content. Mere copying of the West and the North will not help the system to improve the quality of education. If one evaluates consciously the teaching learning practices adopted in many of our higher learning institutions, the major weakness in the system could be easily indentified. With a open mind one has to ask a question whether our educational system is truly of building the skill and knowledge of the students to enable them to be resourceful persons needed to tasks and assignments in various sectors. There is yet another question we have forgotten in the new context. Are we really preparing them as responsible citizens through the process of education in our institutions? For the above question one may not give direct answer.[9]

We have seen in the past some of the teachers in the higher learning institutions have produced outstanding scholars. During those days there was no NAAC, there was no academic audit, no attendance and yet they produced talented students from the institutions. The students came out from the academic institutions were with self-confidence. At one point of time some of the students have expressed that they need only self-confidence that they can lead a life with their own strength, capacity and capability as the students in the West. In such a way, students have to be prepared in the higher learning institutions. No one has to ask whether students from higher learning institutions are coming out with self-confidence despite these accountability measures is yet another question to be answered. We find variations in terms of institutional capacity structurally and functionally and hence one will find variations among the products of these institutions.

Yet another aspect one has to view seriously whether the knowledge, skill and capacity imparted in the system has got any relevance to the life of the stakeholders. We have enormous technologies and vast knowledge bases which are to be used in our educational institutions have not been used because of the system driven cosmetic practices. The changes are fast, but they are to be assimilated and internalized unless otherwise they are mere forms and symbols. The technology developed to enhance the teaching and learning capacity has been used to interact with the best minds in the world has to be used. The institutional location has lost its significance because of the advent of the sophisticated technology for interaction with anyone in any county in the world. Best practices and best minds can be brought to the benefits of the students and for which institutional linkages and availability of the technologies are the imperatives. By doing so many of the institutional deficits could be overcome. Best course and programme design could be prepared with the help of the best experts available in the world without inviting them physically to our places. But our teachers have open mind to change ourselves to the changing context. Despite the presence of accountability procedures and mechanisms if quality is not achieved in our educational institutions, a new set of mechanisms have to be found out. If well established accountability system has not yielded good results in terms of production of quality human power, some other mechanisms have to be found out.

Conclusion

No doubt, the educational institutions have to reposition themselves to meet the new requirements in the world, country and the region. It means educational institutions have to meet the demands of the market and the society and for which new programmes, new courses have to be evolved and they are to be imparted organically. It is an imperative that the existing academic programmes have to be carried out with a rigour to produce the quality manpower suitable to the market. To do this exercise the system has to be geared up and rigour has to be infused in the process. To meet the new demands and requirements, the teachers have to reorient and reposition themselves in the system and its functioning. Total work culture has to be changed. The teachers have to reorient themselves and work in the demands of the stakeholders namely the students. To do the exercise, teachers have to connect themselves with the sectors which absorb the products of the higher learning institutions. The academic programmes have to be fine tuned to meet the labour requirements, whether it is skill labour or knowledge labour of the sectors. It is nothing, but preparation of the workforce to the market from the academic institutions. Hence, teachers are more accountable to the students rather than on the system in which they work. The technologies which have been developed in the world have to be used to upgrade the quality of education. Enough steps have to be taken to improve the quality of teaching and learning to meet the requirements of the students and thereby to meet the requirements of the labour market. To do the above job an instrument is fixed in the system. The instrument is called accountability. The accountability system has to be established organically as it was done in the US and Europe. But in India accountability system is established mechanically. This has to be changed. The present accountability system has to be made downward and not upward. To do the above, the stakeholders have to be involved in the process. In the process of repositioning institutions, the main stakeholders the students have to be involved and due importance is being given to their needs and their views on this subject. By doing so the higher learning institutions have to slowly move from generality to specificity. It moves from supply to demand. By this the higher learning institutions move from teacher centric to students centric. To achieve the above the accountability system has to be changed. The present accountability system is to satisfy the funding agency. It is always a financial audit and it has been to some extent changed to academic audit which is also teacher centric and not student centric. The whole academic accountability system has to be looked at from the perspective of social needs. Whether the knowledge created in the higher learning institution is meeting the social requirements and equally the human power created by the learning institutions are really meeting labour market requirements. In the process needs of the students have to be addressed and that also with the effective and active engagement of the students. Finally, one indicator has to be tested whether students passing out from the higher learning institutions are going with self-confidence. In the whole process of the transformation could be made with the active and positive engagement of every stakeholder without disrupting the entire system by making the transformative process joyful and meaningful with the sense that everybody is working in the process for the benefits of the communities and societies as it has been in vogue for the three decades in the West. It has to be done in an organic way and consciously for the benefit of everyone.

Notes and References

1. Creation of NAAC, IQAC, and JQC, and preparation of Self-Study Report, Academic Audit Report, Self-Evaluation Report, and Student Evaluation Report are the new institutional mechanisms and the processes.
2. Establishment of International Network of Quality Assurance Agencies in Higher Education (INQAAHE).
3. Altbach, P.G. (2001), "Higher Education and the WTO: Globalization run amok" *International Higher Education*, 23, pp. 2-4.
4. Rhodes, G. and Sporn, B. (2002), "Quality Assurance in Europe and the US: Professional and Political Economic Framing of Higher Education Policy", *Higher Education*, 43:3, pp. 355-390.
5. Huigman Jeroen and Currie Jan, (2004), "Accountability in Higher Education: Bridge over Troubled Water?" *Higher Education*, 48: 4C, December, pp. 525 -551.
6. Annual report of the FCCI (2012), in all CII conferences the main speakers lamented upon the poor quality of students turned out from Higher Learning Institutions in India.
7. Palanithurai, G. (2013), *Social Relevance of Higher Education in India*, New Delhi: Concept Publishing Company Pvt. Ltd.
8. Meera Siva (2014), "How to Train Your Population", *Business Line*, 5th August.
9. Arup Majaratna, (2014), "Invasion of Educational Universes by Neo-Liberal Economic Thinking: A Civilization Casualty?" *Economic and Political Weekly*, Vol. XLIX, No. 37, 13th September.

4
Interface between Academia and Policy Community

Introduction

A prominent faculty in National University of Educational Planning and Administration, New Delhi asked a question to me after my presentation on "Decentralization in Educational Governance in India" in a National Policy Seminar held at New Delhi on 16th February, 2015 which prompted me to write this chapter. The question is why our governments are not interested in creating more number of research institutions to do research on the critical issues of development at grassroots; and why there is no meaningful and organic relationship between the policy community and academics? The implied meaning of the question is why governments are not interested in listening to the academics of higher learning and research institutions for policy-making and decision-making. The assumption is that at present there is no direct and systematic relationship between the higher learning institutions and the policy community. In the same way yet another Professor from National Council for Applied Economic Research asked me about the nature of relationship between the academia and the policy-makers and administration when I prepared a policy note on the report prepared by him on "Decentralization and Rural Development". He posited the question with a proposition that despite evidenced based research reports the academic community from the mainstream higher learning institutions could not penetrate into the decision-making and policy-making system systematically and organically. Yet another officer from the State Planning Commission, Government of Tamil Nadu has raised this issue to me when I made a presentation in a meeting organized by the State Planning Commission at Chennai. The question he asked is why there is no organic linkage between the higher learning institutions and policy-planning boards in this country. He specifically mentioned that there are capable and skilled academics in the universities, but they are not connecting themselves with the policy-planning boards. There are many social and economic issues which affect millions of people in our country need to be researched. But it does not take place in quantum. Even if such a kind of research is being done in higher learning institution, the researchers do not connect themselves with policy community. No dearth of higher learning institutions in this country and they do research in huge volume. They are meant for producing research degrees so as to make the individuals eligible to get a job in academic institution or for their promotion in their career. Adequate literature has been developed on many socially relevant issues. Yet they are not being used by the policy planners at Government level or at the stakeholders level either at industry or at community. When question has been asked to the academics about the interface between policy community and academia, without any hesitation they used to argue that the policy community has got a hesitation to interact with academic community. When officials have been asked to ponder over on this subject they argue that the academics mostly skip the policy dimension in their research as they will be subjected to policy scrutiny from the perspective of reality. Apart from the above, there is an accusation by the academic community against the policy community that the institutions which are involved in knowledge creation and dissemination are not properly guided through the policy and it is a total disregard shown by the policy community to the knowledge institution.[1] These questions and observations compelled me to ponder over these problems and issues.

Background

To understand the problem one has to look at the structure and function of the higher learning institutions in India. Basically, the higher learning institutions are autonomous in designing academic programmes and research activities. But on financial governance they are under the regulations of the governments. The private higher learning institutions are so autonomous in designing academic and research programmes and financial management, but they are under overall framework of governance as stipulated by the policy framework of the governments both Central and State. Nowhere, it is stated that what are the essential and obligatory functions and what are the discretionary functions of the higher learning institutions.[2] Higher learning institutions have assumed certain responsibilities based on the funding pattern. Funding agencies have stipulated certain conditions for funding and spending and based on the above, the higher learning institutions have organized their activities. Beyond that there were no mandatory functions stipulated in the statutes. All are recommendatory in nature. As a result, the committee constituted to review the UGC has come to the conclusion that it failed miserably in its functions. In India under the category of higher learning institutions one will find Universities, Deemed Universities, Research Institutions and Colleges. Today in our country we have 745 universities, 39,000 colleges, 11,000 research institutions (number varies from report to report). Essentially, higher learning institutions have obligatory functions namely research and teaching. Obligatory functions came through funding. In order to strengthen both research and teaching, and outreach or extension is made discretionary function.[3] It is a voluntary work not through funding. When we use the term outreach or extension it refers to linkage with end users or stakeholders. It is interpreted differently from different schools of thought. It varies from era to era. There is no uniformity or congruence in the meaning of the term extension or outreach. Students and teachers in higher learning institutions have to connect themselves with the actual community which uses the knowledge created in the higher learning institutions by the joint efforts of the students and the teachers. Essentially, all the three functions are core functions and mandatory for higher learning institutions if the leaders and teachers of the institutions are sensitive, committed and concerned about the society.[4] The assumption is the teachers in higher learning institutions are responsible and responsive to the needs of the society. They should not look for direction or order from the above. They are the role models as they are in higher learning institutions as teachers. All the three activities are mutually reinforcing each other and as a result the stakeholders get the advantage and benefit accrues out of it. We have an education policy and in which nowhere it is stated emphatically that all the three dimensions of the role to be discharged by the teachers are imperative and essential responsibilities of the higher learning institutions. As a result, we find higher learning institutions mostly confined to teaching and producing graduates and post-graduates. When graduate and post-graduate students are passing out from uni-dimensional or bi-dimensional institutions their capacity and capability should not be as high as the students passing out from the institutions which are performing the three dimensional roles professionally. Whatever research the higher learning institutions do, they are for career progression. By doing, this type of research, the teachers build their career. Beyond that scholars do not think they are working for knowledge creation or seeking truth. Teachers at present in higher learning institutions do research at least to build their career. Effectively teaching and research are being carried out not in all the universities. From the perception and perspective of the teachers, teaching is the core function. It is not being insisted that research is also a core function. Research is being not done with the intensity as exhibited by the teachers for teaching. When teachers are taking classes in the higher learning institutions, it was treated as discharge of core responsibility. If the teachers are not actively in research, it is not considered as neglect of duty. Thus, research is considered as discretionary function. When the teachers go for promotion, the teachers are being evaluated from the perspective of both teaching and research.

Extension or outreach is not at all referred in the policy document even though it is also a core function. Extension activity is considered as voluntary or discretionary work. Even for career development of teachers it is not considered. In all kinds of evaluation of the performance of teachers, there is no specific evaluation format for evaluating the performance of the teachers in outreach activities. Further, it is not considered as an achievement for promotion of teachers in higher learning institutions. If a teacher is able to help a *Gram Panchayat* for the preparation of budget or planning for development, these facilitative expert works are not considered for promotion. It is a pity that the experts involved in chalking out policy framework for higher education have not given any thought to this dimension. Even if they mention, it is not detailed as teaching or research. For engineering and technology students, the linkage between industry and academia is emphasized. For social science such linkage is not adequately emphasized. While designing academic programmes and fixing area of research nobody thinks seriously their relevance to the society in most of the public institutions. It is a perceived notion that the academic and research activities of the higher learning institutions are not reflecting the realities and thereby there exist a wide gap between the academic institutions and the world of work. Only private institutions design relevant academic programmes, but it is not sure whether the designed academic programmes are effectively carried out with quality so as to make the students employable.

In the same way, while designing research in higher learning institutions, nobody to bother about their relevance. If realistic assessments are made one will come to a conclusion that rarely they do socially relevant research.[5] It is yet another issue, of the scholars who have done socially relevant research, how many of them have taken the output of the research to the policy desk or action task. Very rarely they are taken to the policy or planning or administration or community. Even if they are taken to the policy community, they are not looked at very objectively. If the policy notes and conclusions are supportive of establishment, they are well received otherwise they are not being touched. There are occasions where researchers are being disturbed by the officials as the conclusions and observations made by the researchers through their research are highly critical to the actions of the Government or policies of the government. By seeing this kind of attitude among the bureaucracy and policy community, many of the academics keep themselves away from the policy community. Even many of the socially relevant projects have not communicated the major findings and policy recommendations to the policy-makers. In such a way, our higher learning institutions have been made to function as per the framework of the Government of India and the provincial governments. Further, the corrupt environment has made the higher learning institutions non-accountable to the stakeholders. Having explained the structure and context of the higher learning institutions, it is necessary to explain the policy-making structure of our political system. Though policy-making and decision-making are the prerogative of the authoritative bodies, there should be a process for gaining knowledge input from the knowledge institutions and knowledge community for scientific policy and decision-making. There should be a constant flow of idea input for policy-making and decision-making. But in Indian context, the higher level bureaucracy considers itself as knowledge repository based on their experience. Having said the background of higher learning institution and bureaucracy, I want to elicit the opinion and views of the researchers who are in higher learning institutions on the interface between academic and policy community.

Methodology

One-to-one intensive interaction I had with academics in four places where I met academics from diverse institutions. I met academics in National University of Academic Planning and Administration, New Delhi, Osmania University, Hyderabad,

University of Madras, Chennai and Gandhigram Rural Institute, Gandhigram. I interacted only with the academics from social science discipline. All my interactions during leisure hours after attending the programme for which they assembled. In the Gandhigram Rural Institute I interacted with certain faculty members who had concern for the society. The discussions were very deep and involved. Teachers with whom I had interactions were very seniors trained in the old school of thought. They expressed their concern, opinion and views on the role of higher learning institutions. Further, I interacted with higher level bureaucracy who are involved in policy and decision-making both in Government of India and Government of Tamil Nadu.

Observations

Following are the observations of the academics:

Never the teachers of higher learning institutions had such a orientation that they have to take up socially relevant theme or issue for research as it had been advocated in post-behavioural revolution in the US. Even if they work on socially relevant theme, they do not have a perspective that the findings should be communicated to the relevant stakeholders for appropriate action. Only through relevance and action social science faculty can demonstrate their importance and usefulness to the society.[6] There is an interesting observation made by some of the teachers that even if we do socially relevant research for policy advocacy teachers should have skill and capacity. With the mere conclusion and observation one cannot do policy advocacy. It is a separate professional activity which has to be done professionally. It requires orientation. When many of the civil society organizations are able to do policy advocacy why scholars in social science discipline from the higher learning institutions are not able to do policy advocacy? This was the question which I have raised to many of the academics in the course of discussion. When I quoted my own experience, many of the academics argued that it is because of lack of orientation on the part of the teachers, they are not able to do policy advocacy even though they do socially relevant research. I explained to the academics that I got such orientation from donor agencies when they organized such programmes for academics who undertake projects from those donor agencies. The IDRC a Canadian donor agency has given a premier research institution a research grant to carry out a research on an important theme which is contextually relevant. A well researched document has been brought out by the institution for the donor agency without having a policy note. But the funding agency refused to accept the document without a policy note. Hence, an offer came to me to prepare a policy note. I have prepared it. For this argument many academics informed me that there is no orientation programme for the academics to do policy advocacy. A separate orientation has to be given to the social science academics for policy advocacy.

When I informed that every Ministry in Government of India has got funds for research, and prioritized areas for research why they are not being tapped by the academics in social science discipline is yet another question raised. A few argued that though some of the faculty members taken up studies and submitted reports based on research nothing was taken from those reports for policy-making. All those reports carry only dust. Since, they have earmarked money for research in the Ministry, they are distributing funds for research in higher learning institutions. But while doing so, they have not kept in their system that the research findings are going to help them either in shaping policy or programme or making course correction in the implementation process of schemes and programmes. There is yet another aspect one has to understand from the behaviour of the bureaucracy. There are many scholars in the academic institutions express their opinion freely on many social issues. But the people who are in helm of affairs do not relish the observations of the academics. Sometimes, even the spicy intellectuals in the university system are sidelined and relegated to the background as they are forthright in their views on social issues. They are being looked at contemptuously by the bureaucrats. This is a learning for many of the teachers in higher learning institutions and hence, they will not make observations or comments on the social issues. Many of the academics are scared of the bureaucrats. Our bureaucracy is fully responsible for such a kind of gap between policy-making system and academic institutions. At present, the leaders of the higher learning institutions have been made to behave as subservient to bureaucracy, the academics do not like to go near to bureaucracy or government. These are the strong views emerged in the discussion.

After listening to the above observation I made yet another statement based on my experience in my department. I have undertaken many research studies mostly sponsored by the donor agencies on socially relevant issues. After the submission of reports I circulate the research findings among the media representatives. They are being published in leading newspapers in the regional columns. Of course, I received lot of criticism from many as if I am indulging in anti-establishment works. Against this background I asked why our academics are not taking the research findings to the media? For this question large number of academics argued that it will generate more of controversies and that would affect the career of the scholars and from that perspective the academics have not taken their research findings to the policy community. Many of the academics indicated that due to intolerance of the bureaucrats and politicians over the critical observations made by academics based on their research, high profile academics have lost opportunity to occupy leadership positions in the universities. As a result, the universities could not get leaders and we find more of managers. They are cronies and they do not allow academics to air observations against establishments. In this context expecting the academics to play such a role is a dangerous game. There are a few exceptional individuals in our country who are active and those academics have determined and committed to do the job unmindful of the consequences and they continue to perform the task. Beyond that there is no such active culture of connecting the academics with policy community. Yet another argument has been projected by many of the academics that to make policy advocacy the academics who has got specialization in a particular field well over a period of time can alone do such a kind of advocacy. In India, it is a moot question how many of the academics in higher learning institutions are specializing in a particular field over decades. Not even one fourth of the teachers are specialists in higher learning institutions in India. Recently, the Deputy Chairman of the Niti Aayog made one observation which came in the press. that in India we lack domain experts and in this regard we have to rely on foreign scholars. It is a clear indication that we do not have the concept of specialization. Since, the culture of specialization is not in practice in many of the higher learning institutions, advocacy is not considered as core task or obligatory function. This is the reason why in the evaluation process of the teachers, it does not figure. By quoting the observation of Panagriya, Vice-Chairman of Niti Aayog, many of the teachers are arguing that Government is interested in keeping foreign scholars as advisers and the policy community is very comfortable with the foreigners and not with Indians. Further, the policy community is interested in engaging foreigners in the context of absence of domain experts. Many State Governments in India engaged foreigners as governance experts. This kind of arguments has made the Indian scholars to behave indifferently to some of the important socio-political issues.

Many of the academics argued that in India the higher level bureaucrats have a perception that they are the people highly competent to look at domain issues perspectively and properly as they gained rich experience in governance and administration. There is yet another argument put forwarded by some of the academics that the bureaucrats have heavy risk and hence they are always conscious and cautious, but academics never face such a kind of risk. They make any observation and advice and they never take such a kind of risk. While taking decision or evolving policies the bureaucrats are having heavy risk and the academics do not have such a kind of risk. When academics express opinion and views on policies and decisions, they do not have any risk, but bureaucrats have huge risk.

There is yet another opinion made by some of the academics that one cannot say that there is no consultation process in the government for policy-making or planning. It takes place but at a limited level. Ministries are constituting committees for such purposes and Planning Commissions both at the Centre and the State are constituting working groups and task forces, for every plan and in which academics have been nominated. Reports have been prepared by them and they are taken into consideration by the policy-makers. I served in many committees of the State government and Central Government on rural local governance issues. Large numbers of committees I have served in the last twenty years. Many academics argued with me that this kind of experience is exceptional and not the rule of in regular practice.

In this country there are two set of academics, one set of academics have developed passion and commitment for teaching and research. Unmindful of the consequences they continuously carryout research and publish the findings. When they are critical of government policies and decisions they are being looked at contemptuously. There is yet another group follow the establishment as they find in every movement careerism. Government is not serious in positioning higher learning institutions in firm footing as in the Western countries. There is yet another strange view echoed by some of the academics while we were in discussion. Knowledge creation and dissemination are the core functions of higher learning institutions theoretically, but in practice, it is only knowledge dissemination function in producing students is being performed. Beyond that there is no serious knowledge works performed by our academics.[7]

There is yet another argument posited by the teachers that globalization has brought series of problems which need investigation. A new set of agenda is needed for action research which is totally missing as government pays little attention on action research.[8] Only some donor agencies concentrate on the critical issues of development and for which they provide funding for action research. There are certain institutions constantly consulted by the governments for policy-making and decision-making. They are few in number. Institutions like Tata Institute of Social Sciences, Institute of Rural Management, Anand, Indian Institute of Public Administration and others are being consulted periodically by the policy-makers. Apart from the above there are a few scholars who have contributed immensely from the university systems have also been consulted periodically. But the whole consultation process is not so systematic and organic. They are not visible also.

A group of academics argues that the academics, though they do research do not have confidence in their research findings to be taken to policy corridors as they do research not for solving the problems or create knowledge but to earn credit points for their career progression. If the academics do research with a passion and commitment, constantly they will take the research findings to the policy corridors with confidence. Unmindful of the consequences and controversies it would generate in the public domain, they brought out issues for public discourse.[9]

One group of academics strongly brought to our discussion a key point that teachers in higher learning institutions have been assigned with much teaching load and hence, they do not find time to do meaningful research. If at all they do research, they do it for their career progression and not for any other purpose. They indicated that in a week a teacher has to take at least 18 hours to teaching as per the UGC norms. If he or she is a sincere teacher, he or she has to devote double the hours of teaching for preparation. So, there will not be any time for meaningful research. In higher education system, teachers have not been allowed to concentrate much on meaningful research.

Finally, I interacted with my own colleagues, their responses and reactions were totally new. They told me that the Rajiv Gandhi Chair for Panchayati Raj Studies was created in Gandhigram Rural Institute not by any donor agency or by the UGC or by the Government. It was created by the faculty as it has to work for the people through Panchayati Raj. It was basically designed to do research and conduct training for grassroots leaders and conduct outreach programmes. It has to stand on its own by its performance. It has done all the works and drew the attention of all the bilateral and multilateral agencies. All kinds of socially relevant issues have been taken for research and brought out valuable reports.[10] They have been taken to the policy community. When they have not acted on the reports, the reports have been taken to media. Further, popular articles have been written in popular vernacular newspapers on social issues. The Rajiv Gandhi Chair for Panchayati Raj Studies in collaboration with a vernacular newspaper a supplement was published every Monday for the benefit of the rural masses about rural development schemes and Panchayati Raj Governance. It was well appreciated by all. Yet we have faced lot of problems internally and through officials simply because we were critical of the establishments. Having experienced such a hardship how one can expect the academics to play a critical role on development issues. It is not a Western country to appreciate free flow of ideas, where even dissent voice is heard with respect. It is an accepted fact that the university academics have to work for well-being of the people through the three dimensional works namely teaching, research and outreach. But working with policy community is a most dangerous game. While serving in government funded institutes, teachers have to go with government.

Further, I interacted with a few government officials who are at secretary level both in Government of India and at provincial level. It is the major point emerged from the discussion I had with them. The policy community is facing tough time as they find scarcity of domain experts from the academic institutions to get needed input for policy and decision-making. Academics are carrying out reach not with the objective of finding solution to the problems faced by the communities. Very rarely one could see such a kind of academics in the university system. Sometimes one could find such a kind of research in civil society organizations. It is perceived notion among the civil servants about the academics and academic institutions that they are away from social realities. This notion was not crude but foreign scholars are to the point and they have more in-depth details about the issues and that is why government is interested to work with foreigners. They cite Robert chambers for this matter. Hence, Government relies on foreign consultants also. Government is always willing to consult with anyone who provides the needed input. There are channels to send ideas, views and observations for the policy advocates. Even through mails, government officials are getting views, opinions and observations based on the research conducted by institutions and individuals on policies, programmes and schemes. It is to be understood that by giving some input based on research one cannot expect they will be taken to policy framework. If they are valuable and useful no one will reject it. Government always welcomes opinions, views, observations and comments. There is yet another argument projected by the officials. They argued that research is not the prerogative of the academics alone. A farmer can do research in his or her field. A vendor can do research in his or her job. Research is being done by various agencies based on their needs and mandates. Many of the innovative ideas for governance and administration came from market and civil society organizations. Hence, one cannot presume that academics are alone doing research. All those points have been made by the officials.

Conclusion

In the process of discourse with many senior academics of different universities on the interface between policy community and academia, it is found that teachers have expressed their willingness to connect themselves with policy community provided a well structured institutional mechanism is in place for intensive, organic and systematic interaction. The whole process should be put in a systematic mode with organic linkages. It should take place in a democratic academic and research setting. Further, academics should have clear orientation to do policy advocacy.

Researchers in social science need such a kind of orientation to do policy advocacy. It is felt that in the absence of research policy and outreach policy in higher learning institutions all such activities are *ad hoc* in nature. Exceptionally well qualified academics who have specialization on the development issues at the grassroots are being treated as anti-establishment and anti development and such a kind of treatment prevent many from connecting themselves with policy community. This syndrome has to go from the policy corridors. A well meaning comprehensive education policy will address all the issues working against the relationship between academia and policy community.

Notes and References

1. Pushpa, M. Bhargava, 2015, "For a renaissance in Indian S&T", *The Hindu*, 28th March, p. 10.
2. Agarwal, Pawan, 2007, "From Kothari Commission to Pitroda Commission", *Economic and Political Weekly*, 17th February, 2007.
3. Palanithurai, G., 2009, "Rural Universities in the Era of Globalization", *University News*, Vol. 74, No. 33, August.
4. Palanithurai, G. 2006, "Larger Role of Academics in Rural Human Life", *University News*, Vol. 47, No. 16, April.
5. Palanithurai, G., 2012, *Social Relevance of Higher Learning Institutions*, New Delhi: Concept Publishing Company Pvt. Ltd.
6. G. Palanithurai, *2007, Globalization: Concerns at the Grassroots and How to Address them?*, Gandhigram: Rajiv Gandhi Chair for Panchayati Raj Studies.
7. Shiv Visvanathan, 2015, "A New Public Policy for a New India: *The Hindu*, 6th April.
8. Milind Sohomi, 2015, "The University and Development Agenda", *Economic and Political Weekly*, Vol. L, No. 11, 14th March, pp. 19-21.
9. Preeti Sampat, 2015, "Growth for a few and loss for many", *The Hindu* 28th March, p. 11; Vanita Leah Falca and Jasmeet Khamuja, 2015, "India's Unrealized Maternity Entitlements", *The Hindu*, 28th March, p. 11.
10. Palanithurai, G., 2008, *Ten Years of Experience in Decentralization*, Gandhigram: Rajiv Gandhi Chair for Panchayati Raj Studies.

5

Non-seriousness in Learning and Teaching in Social Science

A Micro-Analysis

Introduction

An important issue, which is being faced by the teachers of social science in many of the higher learning institutions located in the rural areas, is non-seriousness of one section of the students who are pursuing undergraduate and post-graduate programmes in social sciences in the past ten years. The teachers are able to perceive the poor capacity and capability of the students who are joining social science stream either out of compulsion or out of no other choice is the reason for their non-seriousness. They are below the level of an expected standard and as a result they are not serious in their studies. Further, they are not drawn towards these programmes out of their own interest and passion, but because of compulsions and circumstances. General impression has been created among the stakeholders that social science programmes are not professionally oriented to specific jobs. Like professional courses, the social science students cannot expect job offer in the campus itself. After getting their degree they have to search for jobs and the institutions which are offering social science programmes are not giving assurance for jobs as Engineering and Business Schools. Hence, they do not envisage any hope on these programmes for their future career prospects. Above arguments are being projected casually by the teachers based on their own analysis and experience. But one has to go deeper into those arguments as to what extent the arguments have got veracity and validity. Yet one has to move into the reality at the ground. The reality is that one section of the students in social science programmes in higher learning institutions is non-serious in their studies. While making such a comment, it does not mean that all the students of technology, science and medicine are serious always. Since, we see this problem in social science, we try to understand and analyze the factors responsible for it and to correct the course for making the students in social science programme more serious. High profile students in social science are able to see the fine job opportunities available for social science programmes. They find jobs in governing institutions, administrative arrangements, civil society organizations, business organizations, media and other agencies. Students who got degrees in development administration and social work are in corporate world. Our students (M.A. Development Administration) are in bilateral and multilateral agencies and apart from the above they are in corporate companies looking after corporate social responsibility activities. Academics in high profile universities are lamenting that they are not able to find quality researchers for project works despite they pay more than Rs. 30,000 per month. Here, it is to be underlined that production of Ph.D. from the universities is on the increase. From the above scenario one can come to a conclusion on the face value of it that students are interested in getting certificate not in learning. Many of the good research programmes need good researchers from social science. But in the market we could not find quality manpower for research. Further, it is to be made clear that this non-seriousness is pertinent to only one segment of the students of social science. Before moving into the analysis of the issue one has to understand the conditions of entire social science teaching and research in India. Adequate evidences from the commissioned reports argue that social science teaching and research are qualitatively and quantitatively poor.[1] There is no professionalism in the teaching and research. As a result we could not produce quality manpower for the need of the society. Against this background we look at this issue.

Mandate from Above

Government of India has fixed the target for enrollment of students in higher learning institutions in order to compete with other parts of the world in quality human power production with an objective of participating in knowledge economy and stabilizing the economic growth of the country.[2] Here one has to see the objective that it is only to accelerate economic growth not the well-being of the community. Hence, institutions are geared up to enroll more number of students. So necessarily, we have to increase the seats in all the Programmes. Now, we are doubling the enrollment rate. While increasing the enrollment rate no one is bother to look at the facilities available and the availability of teachers. Without increasing the facilities and teaching strength, increasing the enrollment rate is mere number game. One cannot expect in this process quality manpower from the higher learning institutions. While mandating the institutions to increase the enrollment our administrative and executive heads of the institutions are making observation that for social science programmes we require only classrooms to accommodate students beyond that we need not worry about other things. In such a way our administrative heads have perceptions and understandings. In the process of globalization of economy more number of students are joining only in professional courses as market demands more number of graduates for industries and service sector. Here also it is to be noted that the students coming out from the technical institutions are not able to meet the required qualification as expected by the industry and service sectors. Industry and service sectors loudly argue that they are not able to get the quality manpower needed to them.

One segment of social science and humanities students are not evincing keen interest in their studies and they are really compelled to join in such courses. Those who are really interested and serious in pursuing social science programmes out of passion are moving abroad or joining in premier institutions which take only limited number of students. They find learning environment in those institutions. Moreover, students who are joining the social science programmes in conventional public institutions are not aware of the job potentials in the market. Further social science and humanity programmes are considered by the political class as non-viable and non-utility courses. Hence, adequate attention is not paid to equip the programmes and the institutions which are offering the social science programmes. As a result one will find non-seriousness among one segment of students in social science programmes. From the above argument, one will conclude easily that quality manpower production is a daunting task.

Status in Tamil Nadu

Normally in Tamil Nadu barring a few premier institutions, universities are not getting adequate students for social science programmes. Government colleges with subsidized fee structure they get students. Beyond that for social science under graduate and post-graduate programmes one will not find adequate students. Even if one finds adequate number of students for social science one will not find intelligent, studious, hardworking and committed students. Students will not come to social science on their own as even for a just pass in school examinations in Tamil Nadu one can get engineering and medical seats provided one has got money. Even economically poor students can get bank loan for technical education. For the past several years several thousand seats are vacant in engineering colleges in Tamil Nadu. Hence, finding students for social science is the difficult task in the universities and colleges. When we get students through the efforts of the teachers, the students who get admitted in the institution are non-serious in their studies. Against this background we run social science programmes in universities. All public higher learning institutions are facing the same problem of this nature. Heavy concentration of technical institutions have tilted the balance towards technology by negating social sciences and humanities in Tamil Nadu. As a result one will find poor quality of graduates coming out from the social science programmes. For governance, administration, research, social work and civil society works we need more professionally qualified manpower. Our higher learning institutions could not produce such quality manpower through social science programmes. By producing poor quality graduates in higher learning institutions we are transferring the burden to the society. All our failures in public administration, governance, policy-making, and policy and programme implementation are due to poor quality of staff substantially produced from social science programmes. Teachers in social science in higher learning institutions are not introspecting the core issue of quality human power production.

A Micro-Experience

In Gandhigram Rural Institute, we mobilize students for social science programmes during every summer and admit them on the basis of merit. Since, they are drawn from the rural areas and from Tamil medium stream barring a few, making them to be active in learning is very difficult. They join the social science programme not with enthusiasm and hope as other students who are pursuing engineering programmes. Most of them are from Tamil medium. They come with a set of core learning disability and of them communication disability is one. This syndrome is because of the unwritten policy of our Government of Tamil Nadu that students from first to tenth standard should be allowed to move easily from one class to another till they reach the tenth. To some extent it has reduced the high rate of drop-outs. But quality is compromised.

Shaping them as products to the labour market through these processes is the toughest job to be done in higher learning institutions. Yet struggle is going on to make them saleable. We adopt different methods and approaches to make them academically engaged. We have placement bureau, career and counselling cell, free coaching centre for students who are preparing for competitive examinations. The faculty of English is giving communicative skill course for a short duration to the students who are weak in communication skill. Apart from the above coaching centres, there are nine clubs mostly for student's activities coordinated by nine teams of teachers. They conduct varieties of activities and programmes by involving the students and experts with the aim of increasing the skill and capacity of the students. In order to enhance the understanding of the rural reality, field-work, extension work, internship, field placement and village placement programmes are conducted continuously. Those activities are in the time tables of the respective faculty and in every department teachers are in charge of the above extension and co-curricular activities. If all the opportunities are being used by the students, 80 per cent to 90 per cent of the students can get placement opportunity easily. It is not happening as we expect. We are analyzing the reasons for poor placement profile and non-seriousness of the students on the social science programmes. Non-seriousness of the students on studies is due to various factors and of which one is obvious and predominant that neither the parents nor the stakeholders are clear about the focused purpose of pursuing the social science programmes. Both have vague idea about its saleability. Further the social science programmes in public institutions are being conducted in a non-professional way. As a result it becomes a ritual of taking classes, conducting tests and issuing certificates. There is no substantial academic engagement in many public institutions.[3]

I have been in the process of identifying an appropriate strategy to make social science programmes more attractive, sealable and professional. In this process in our department (Department of Political Science and Development Administration) instead of offering M.A. Political Science or M.A. Public Administration, we have introduced M.A. Development Administration with a special focus on development management. We prepare person power for development agencies as middle level managers. By seeing the moderate success we have introduced yet another programme called M.A. Governance and Development. In India barring a few institutions social science programmes are not being offered professionally and seriously.

But recently I have noticed a new venture among the poor students who are in the portals of higher education while pursuing social science programme. From the venture, I tried to locate the issue and its reasons. Till then I used to accuse the students as they are not serious in their studies. But the new venture gives hope that the present day youth have developed aspiration to achieve development and for which they determine to work hard. Really the teachers have to concentrate much on the students apart from going to the regular classes for teaching. Students require personal attention of the teachers not only for studies, but also for career guidance and counselling. But it is not available for students in many of the public institutions at present. Generally, there is a perception that students who are pursuing social science and humanities programme are non-serious. Students coming from the poorest segments of the society for social science programme are not only non-serious but also problematic. This myth is broken when I moved closely with students who are pursuing social science programmes from the poor families in our institute. The present day youth those who are coming to the higher learning institutions from poor socio-economic background are sincere in pursuing their duties and responsibilities and managing themselves on their own. They perform their duties and responsibilities through a new venture. The new venture is "earn while you learn".

An Event

When I was in the classroom a few students were sleeping in the last bench and I have noticed it. Once the class was over, I asked them about the reason for their sleepy mood. The answer was shocking to me. They told me that in the previous day they went for a work to earn money for their educational expenses. Further, I probed them about the work they have done in the previous day. They worked in a catering service as assistants to cook and waiters. For a marriage function the caterers have taken contract for cooking and serving food to the guests. In the contract catering service our students served as workers. Their answer did not stop with this, further they told me that there are students going for painting work regularly to earn money. There are students going for masonry work, and night watchman work. All the students who are going for work are from the ultra poor families. They are going for the work to earn money with the knowledge of their parents. I asked yet another serious question as why are you not serious about studies? When you are going for such a kind of works how do you concentrate on your studies? Are you not interested in studies? They told me that they are not able to predict their future with the social science degree. One thing they made it clear that they should not be a burden to their family. Both the parents and the students did not have adequate information about the academic programmes. They did not have adequate resources to join in engineering colleges. Their marks are very minimum. Hence, they opted for social science programmes. Their communicative ability is very minimum.

But one asset they keep with them that is their internal strength. Their internal strength is very high. They developed hope about their future. Their passion for struggle is very high. They want to stand on their own. They get scholarship. They did not get money from their parents. Only at the time of admission, they get money from their parents and for all other expenditures they earn and spend. They further told me that they joined Gandhigram Rural Institute as it has flexible field based system of education and the entire institute has developed a perspective to work for the marginalized and poor. It is not their perception, but it was the perception of their parents. Teachers are lenient towards the students of the poor families that enabled them to do the above jobs.

In fact I interacted with many such students in our campus mostly from social science stream.[4] When I interacted with them I used to make one serious comment. The students are not taking the educational programme so serious. Whether attending classes or taking seminar, or writing assignments students have not evinced keen interest as students evinced in technical institutions. For all the questions they replied that seriousness depends on both sides. Teachers and students have to interact closely. The whole educational process is not enjoyable. The teaching of the teachers is not enjoyable, how can one expect seriousness among the students. Classrooms are fully occupied by the teachers. There is no space for the students. Teachers never consider the diverse background of the students. For them students are the same. In fact, understanding of the teachers about the students is very poor. These are the observations of the students. Further, the students should feel that after attending and getting certificate from the programme they will be placed in such a position in such an organization. There is no guarantee for the job. The students going for technology entertain hope that they will be placed somewhere. In reality they are also not getting it. Whereas the students who are joining the social science programme do not have any hope at all. In which segment they get job opportunity is not known to them. The students who are pursuing social science academic programmes relied on hope only in their skills. While pursuing their programmes they do lot of works for earning. There is yet another segment of students who are

Table 5.1: Work details of the students

Sl. No.	*Nature of Work*	*Average Earning Per Day*	*Average Days Per Month*	*Per Month Earning*
1.	Helper to electricians	350	6 days	2100
2.	Waiter in catering	450	5 days	2250
3.	Mason	600	6 days	3600
4.	Kitchen assistant	350	6 days	2100
5.	Gardener	250	4 days	1000
6.	Night watchman	200	8 days	1600
7.	Toilet cleaner	300	6 days	1800
8.	Helper to mason	250	6 days	1500
9.	Helper to carpenter	250	6 days	1500
10	Call driver	600	4 days	2400
11.	Painting	500	4 days	2000

Source: Computed.

pursuing the social science programme go for higher studies. They do research or join in either academic and research institutions or development organizations.

The students of the poor families go for garden work, watchman work, painting, masonry work, helping carpenters as assistant, helper in construction work, assisting electricians, drivers and some of them are going for toilet cleaning works. The details of the work, earning per day, earning per month are shown in Table 5.1.

When I interacted with the students they gave reply to many of my questions and I have tabulated the responses as shown in Table 5.1. When I shooted another question as, why you have not pursued vocational education instead of academic stream? Their reply was that the academic degrees will increase their social status and the skills they acquire will help for them to earn their livelihood. The students who are going for different *ad hoc* jobs are not having adequate certificates to do the job. Everyone knows that in India anyone can do any job as there is no regulatory mechanism. Hence, these students acquired certain skills from their parents and perform the job. For some of the jobs a few days orientation is enough. Some of the students feel that there should be good blend of some vocational skills with academic programmes. They argue that they are in need of some skill sets which provide job opportunities to them. They further reiterated that if the students are going out from the universities with certificates for both academic programmes and skill sets, their probability of getting employment opportunity is very high.[5]

What they Need?

When I interacted with students I found enormous amount of aspiration in them to achieve development more particularly to acquire material things and for which they wanted to work. Many of the students have realized that their family is in poverty. They want to come out from poverty by making use of his or her education. Many felt that to claim their self-dignity they want to lead a decent life and for which they want to acquire certain material things. But at the same time they are searching for opportunities to work and to earn money. They find opportunities only at the lower level. They go for work and earn and they are not a burden to their families. At the same time they want to earn continuously and for which they are searching for skills which are not readily available in the university system. They come to university system to acquire a degree. But according to their desire they are not able to excel in academic programmes. At the same time by this academic degree they get social status. Yet they need skills to enhance their employability. They have no hesitation to work and do any job. They want to do it more professionally. They need a skill set while interacting with them they indicated that they want to learn driving car, truck and other technical heavy vehicles. They want to learn computer operation with minimum skills. They need some elementary skills to work in hospitals. Some of them are interested in learning catering technology. They know a few items of food variety preparation. They want to go out with a

Table 5.2: Needed Skills Set as per the Demand of the Students

Sl. No.	*Skills Needed*	*Sl. No.*	*Skills Needed*
1.	Car Driving	17.	Gardening
2.	Truck Driving	18.	Communication
3.	Earth Mover Driving	19.	Secretarial assistance
4.	AC Mechanic	20.	Statistical analysis
5.	Compounder in Hospital	21.	Report writing for newspapers
6.	Computing	22.	Natural beautification
7.	Nursing	23.	Artificial beautification
8.	Old Age Care	24.	Hair clipping
9.	Event Management	25.	Sales and service
10.	Plumbing	26.	Cell phone repairing
11.	Electrician	27.	Photography
12.	Fitter	28.	Legal assistance
13.	Turner	29.	Masonry
14.	Hospitality	30.	Accounting
15.	Catering	31.	Painting
16.	Carpentry		

Source: Computed.

certificate or a degree with a few skills which are having adequate demand in their vicinity. They suggested that every university should have a community college where skills can be learnt and in the regular university classes academic programmes can be learnt. There should be flexibility between the programmes of the regular university and the programmes of the community college. They want academic programme in the morning and skill learning in the evening.

Table 5.3: Demand for Soft Skills by the Students

Sl. No.	*Skills Needed*
1.	Personality Development
2.	Communication skill
3.	Presentation skill
4.	Leadership skill
5.	Career Planning skill
6.	Problem Solving skills
7.	Contact Resolution skills
8.	Critical Thinking skills
9.	Mentoring skills
10.	Public Speaking skill
11.	Development Reporting skill
12.	Proposal Writing skill

Source: Computed.

Box 5.1: Gurukula System

The purpose of establishing '*Gurukula* System' in our university (Gandhigram Rural Institute) is to establish an intimate relationship between the students and the teachers apart from the class hours contact. It enables the teachers to understand the student's socio-economic background, their aspirations and their problems. In the same way, students can have mentors and they seek guidance help and counselling from the *guru*. Every class has got a *guru*. It helps the institute to solve many of the student's problems collectively and paves the way for getting the students involved in their studies with a hope that they have support base. The mechanical way of keeping relationship in the classroom between the students and the teachers will be changed to establish organic way of relationship between students and teachers through the *Gurukula* system. To perform the above job the teachers should have commitment, passion and love for that work. Otherwise teachers will make that into a class room discussion. Many of the things which cannot be discussed in formal classroom setting can be discussed with the teachers by the students in the informal *Gurukula* setting.

Box 5.2: Development is Struggle

A boy pursuing M. Phil. degree told me that he has a set of skills and they are being used during leisure hours to earn money. He keeps the money for his studies and expenditures. Whenever his mother demands money for family household expenditure he used to part with money. At the same time he continuously works by using his skills. He can drive a car, he can use computer, he can manage a garden, and he can act as a mason to fix tiles. When I interacted with him I came to know that his brothers also developed such a kind of practice. All the three brothers are educated and for their education their skills helped a lot. Here, it is to be noted that this boy had no hesitation to tell anyone that his family background is poor and he is earning for his education. But at the same time he felt that the society has not changed its perception. The society continue to look at the poor students differently and not on par with the others. Hence, he wants to earn and stand on his own.

Box 5.3: Teacher's Eye Contact

Whenever I met students, I could gather lot of stories about them. I could get the details of their difficulties with which they pursue academic programmes. By interacting with them continuously one can motivate them and many of the occasions students coming from the poor families are in frustration. By our constant interaction and movement with them enable them to get empowerment. Normally, the students from the poor families that too from the marginalised families expect that the eyes of the teachers should be on them while the teachers are in the class. Many of the students told me that many of the teachers never turned towards them as they are ugly, not handsome, black and not in good dress. Teacher's eye contact is being seriously viewed by the students who belong to marginalised groups. By their teachers eye contact many of the students can be drawn towards the teacher and it will help them to empower themselves. This fact made me to look at the students in the classroom properly. The eye contact will be on all the students.

Box 5.4: A Teacher's Initiative for the Poor Students

A teacher is helping nearly forty girl students by paying Rs. 7000/- to pay for examination and tuitions fee from a corpus developed by the development workers of Netherland. The teacher has approached the individuals when they visited the university. The Netherland friends have agreed to help them. They set-up a corpus fund and it was deposited in the nationalized banks. The interest accrued on the investment will be distributed. Annually after getting applications, they are being screened and they will be paid from the interest amount accrued out of their deposit. A Gandhian thought professor out of his own interest after seeing the plight of the girls coming from the poor families to higher learning institutions approached his foreign friends coming from Netherland regularly to India for development work. The whole scheme is with the teacher. He used to collect application and process the same and while selecting candidates for the scheme a member from the Netherland team come and participate. On an average thirty to forty girls from the poorest families are getting benefits out of the scheme.

Box 5.5: Clubs for Students

Teachers take extra responsibility of the students in different kinds of activities according to the students' wish. For all such activities clubs have been formed and students have been enrolled as members. University gives facilities and financial assistance to conduct such programmes. The clubs are as follows:

1. Trekking club
2. Adventure club
3. Bird watchers club
4. Sky gracing club
5. Movie club
6. Gardening club
7. Campus beautification club
8. Photographic club
9. Personality and Leadership club
10. Cultural and Music club
11. Environmental club
12. Ecology club

Box 5.6: Teacher's Initiative to help for Higher Studies

A few teachers joined together and created a corpus fund. Annually, a few students are helped for their studies only through this corpus fund. The amount is distributed to deserving students for remitting tuition fee or examination fee. The corpus was initially created by the liberal donation of a teacher. A student from a marginalised family got a help from his teacher. He did his masters, M. Phil. and Ph.D. and joined in a prestigious institute as faculty. He returned back the money to his teacher and asking his teacher to have a fund to help such a kind of students as he got from him. This made many teachers to contribute for corpus to help the deserving students to pursue their higher studies.

Box 5.7: Academic Social Responsibility

Having understood the extreme implications of poverty, a few teachers have joined together to provide breakfast to the students who are coming to the university without having breakfast in their homes. The teachers are distributing coupons every month to the students. The needy students have to collect the coupons and gave them to the canteen and have food. The whole arrangement is made silently without any advertisement. I came to know through a student of mine who regularly take breakfast in the canteen. When she came late to the class, I asked her to explain why she is late? She told me that she could not get the breakfast in the canteen in the time. When I asked further she told me that she is getting coupon every month from a teacher and have Tiffin in the canteen. She narrated this issue to me and then I investigated the full details of this help done to the students by a group of our teachers.

Box 5.8: A Struggle for Development

A boy from a poor family continuously working in a catering team as a helper from his school days up to M. Phil. programme in physics. He earns on his own and spend for his studies. He maintained his close relationship with his teachers. They also helped him. For his Ph.D. programme he got his scholarship and pursuing his programme. Till he reached Ph.D. programme he earned through his work and he got substantial amount of money from his teachers. His hard work, determination, unmindful of others perception, good will of the teachers enabled him to come to the level of Ph.D. in physics. These kinds of youths are the models. They struggle continuously for their upward mobility and it is a development struggle.

All the above initiatives are not institutional and mandated by the institution. Some of them are unique exercises practiced in Gandhigram Rural Institute over a period of time. Teachers who have internalized the values do it organically and add value to the system. Many of the activities are initiated by the teachers voluntarily by joining together. I came to know the teachers initiative only from the students while interacting with them as Dean Students Welfare. Those who move with students very closely know the conditions of the students and help them to come up in life. Students from the last rung of the society need the support of the teachers outside the classrooms. The major question is whether the teachers are willing to work with the students outside the classroom. Further students need both skills and knowledge for getting gainful employment and for which the system has to respond to it. There should be a balanced mix of skill and knowledge to gain employment opportunity and for which the system has to take initiative.

Conclusion

Students from the rustic families came with aspirations and they are not able to cope up with the system. Their family conditions made them to earn and stand on their own. Many are in struggle. We call it a development struggle. They have some skills and they make use of the skills available with them. But their skills are not fine tuned and sharpened. Teachers and the institutions are also taking earnest efforts to engage the students and help the students at individual level and collectively. It is not the entire teaching community involve themselves in such a kind of activities to help the students who are in need. The students are much thankful to the teachers. But what they want is a right mix of skills along with knowledge through a system.

Universities and higher learning institutions should have community colleges to offer menu of skills. Students who are pursuing academic programmes in humanities and social sciences should have opportunity to learn a few skills which will increase the opportunity to get jobs in the market. While pursuing academic programmes students hailing from the poorest segment needs monetary assistance that could be created in the university itself or outside the university system. They are ready to work and earn for their studies. To enable them to work and earn while pursuing academic programmes, they need flexibility in timetable. Students argue that they are ready to be in the university up to 2.00 P.M. from morning 8.30. After that they will be freed from the academic assignments.

In the evening they want to go for work. They go for work during Saturday and Sunday. Small works in the university campuses should be given to them and for which they have to be paid. As we have "earn while you learn" scheme in Gandhigram University, every university should have such arrangements. Students need attention from the teachers apart from the class hours and for which "*Gurukula* System" can be organized in every university and an hour can be fixed for such a kind of interaction. Importance of skill education has to be popularized. Every university should have a website with students' profile and it should be linked to employment portals which are maintained by various agencies. Flexible learning arrangement should be in the educational programme of the higher learning institutions. Students from the poor family background need the teachers' help more outside the classrooms. Of course, a few teachers are doing such a kind of work out of their passion. In a country like India, students from the marginalized group need the support of teachers all the time for their emancipation. Seriousness not merely attending classes in learning skills needed to lead a decent dignified life. Hence, seriousness of students in studies depends on how serious the teachers are in helping the students outside the classroom interaction.

Notes and References

1. Pawan Agarwal, 2009, *Indian Higher Education: Envisioning the Future*, New Delhi: Sage Publications, p. 279.
2. M. Anandakrishnan, *"Privatization of Higher Education: Opportunities and Anomalies"* 2006, paper presented at the conference on Privatization and Commercialization of Higher Education organized by NIEPA in New Delhi on 2nd May.
3. G. Palanithurai, 2012, *Social Relevance of Higher Learning Institutions*, New Delhi: Concept Publishing Company Pvt. Ltd., pp. 33-46.
4. Being a Dean, Students welfare, I interacted with students on different occasions and recorded the views and observations of the students on learning environment in the campus.
5. G. Palanithurai, 2013, *"Are the Youth Liability or Asset?"* *Puthiyathalaimurai Kalvi* (in Tamil), Vol. 3, No. 22, 14th January.

6
Skill Development in Higher Learning Institutions
A Micro Analysis

Introduction

Twenty-first century's opportunity for India to achieve greater economic prosperity lies in making use of the youth and the working age population. To utilize this new opportunity demographic dividend effectively India needs to impart adequate and appropriate skills to our youth. India has missed many opportunities in the past but not this as it would create more pressure on the state and society. It requires vision, mission, commitment, strategies, institutions, resources, synergy, political and administrative will and a movement. The task is much complex and assignment is huge and hence to achieve the same leadership is crucial and critical. Leadership from the office of the Prime Minister to a *Gram Panchayat* plays a critical role in transforming India by skilling and empowering our youth population. Everyone at the operational level needs awareness and consciousness and more particularly strategic action with a sense of commitment. At every level, a clear understanding and concrete actions are the imperative need. In India we have a policy[1], a coordination board[2], a framework[3], financial allocation[4], and a target[5] for skilling our youth. And yet we find the whole exercise of skilling our youth and preparing them for a new challenge is tardy and slow.[6] All exercises meant for skilling our youth are moving in a snails pace. There are many stakeholders in this exercise. What we need is more synergetic action by coordinating different agencies and stakeholders. Of all, the end users are the youths in the educational institutions and are to be conscientised. Hence, the present chapter tries to analyze the role of higher learning institutions in skilling the students and how this process of skilling is being viewed by the stakeholders. In this chapter, I am trying to focus on the students coming out from the arts and science stream of higher learning institutions as they constitute still 56 per cent of the total students passing out from the total higher learning institutions.

The Problem

On the one hand we have adequate youth for employment and on the other the market faces shortage of workforce for its transactions in India. This gap between supply and demand of workforce is due to the failure in preparing the youth for labour market. Obviously our youth have not been properly trained in skills needed to the market. Now as our economy grows, to sustain the economy, it is felt that the workforce has to be adequately skilled. Against this background increasing realization has come to all stakeholders that skilling of our youth should become a development movement in India. To transform the youth into a capacitated workforce, youth have to be trained and more particularly in skills needed to the market. While preparing the youth for market adequate care has to be taken to suit the requirements of the market, and by which the skill gap has to be reduced. The skilling process takes place through educational institutions from the school to higher learning institutions. It is a fact to be recognized that in India since independence our education system did not give much attention on the skills. Despite the arguments of M.K. Gandhi on skill based learning, our educational pandits started paying attention on liberal education oriented to acquire knowledge. Adequate opportunities had been given to test the education system evolved by M.K. Gandhi. Even the fourteen Rural

Institutes created for experimenting the Gandhian framework of education have been merged into the liberal education system in India.[7] Realization came at a later stage that skilling is an imperative need and governments took efforts to catch up. This skilling exercise is also for industries and service industries.

Despite the earnest efforts on the part of the educational institutions, the products coming out from the academic institutions are of poor quality in terms of precise skills needed to industry and other sectors. It is more obvious from the lamentations of the business leaders that skill level of our students is poor and unsuited to the industry and service sectors. This is about the conditions of the technical institutions. There is yet another segment in higher learning system called Arts and Science stream which is still predominant in the education sector. In the total human power coming out from the education sector, 56 per cent of them are from the Arts and Science stream.[8] But the students coming out from the arts and science stream do not focus their attention either on industry or service sector for their employment. They rely on government and educational sectors. It is only after globalization their attention was drawn towards industry, and service sectors.

Transforming this segment of the students from arts and science stream into a productive workforce will certainly help the economy to grow, reduce unemployment rate and mitigate the social unrest in the society. But skilling of the students of arts and science stream of higher learning institutions is the difficult and stupendous task and yet it has to be done. Against this background, it is proposed to investigate the skilling process of the students of arts and science stream in conventional universities from the stakeholders' point of view.

Methodology

To get answer to the above questions and objective, a focus group discussion was conducted in a higher learning institution

(Gandhigram Rural Institute–Deemed University, a centrally funded Deemed University located in a rural setting) among the students who are pursuing postgraduate programmes in social sciences. The discussion was about their perception of skills required for the market; the skills needed for them to be made employable and a system and processes needed to this task. The whole discussion was held in different spells and in different settings. While conducting the focus group discussion care was taken to brief the context and issues of skilling youth. While drawing students both boys and girls for discussion care was taken to involve substantial numbers from marginalized communities.

Background

Before coming to analyze the responses of the respondents, it is necessary to give the background of the whole issue of skilling youth. Government of India has realized the potentials of youth and the market and taken the appropriate policy to transform the youth force into a workforce to cater to the needs of the labour market. Elaborate strategies have been worked out to realize the targets. Appropriate institutional supports are sought. Resources have been allocated and for this task financial institution has been created. Prime Minister is coordinating the skill development initiatives in the country through National Council on Skill Development. It fixed the target of skilling 500 million people by 2022. Next to the council, there is a National Skill Development Coordination Board. The role of the board is to work out the strategies to implement the decisions of the Prime Minister's National Council for Skill Development and create comprehensive guidelines to realize the basic objectives of skill development. National Skill Development Corporation has been created. It is a public-private joint venture with 49 per cent equity held by the Government. A large number of initiatives are taken and responsibilities have been entrusted to different agencies to build the skill among the youth to make them as employable labour force. It is a known fact that the present capacity of institution is to train 3.1 million. But 12.8 million people join in labour force in every year.

Here, it is to be seen that 93 per cent of the workforce are in unorganized sector in India. Further, it is to be recognized that skill development takes place both formally and informally. Yet achieving target is problematic one in India. The responsibility lies with different agencies. Central Government, State Governments, educational institutions, industrial houses, civil society organizations and media have responsibilities and they have to discharge their responsibilities in a synergetic way. All those who work in the skill development domain have to work synergistically and systematically to make use of the new opportunities. The whole exercise has to be conducted in a mission mode. Further, they have to work in close coordination with labour market. Apart from the above all, the activities have to be carried out in a sustainable way.

A realistic estimate informs that skill base of the Indian economy is very low compared to developed economies of the world. Vocational training capacity is also low. To manage the above, a new initiative has been taken at the Central Government level. We have skill development policy 2009, National Council for Skill Development, National Skill Development Coordination Board, National Skill Development Council, seventeen Ministries initiatives for skill development, National Skill Development Fund, skill sector council and national vocational education qualification framework. Efforts have been on to coordinate government, industry, trade unions and civil society. In the whole process, a marked departure has been made to pursue the goal of achieving skill development from output to outcome oriented which is considered as significant step in right direction. The role of State governments, industry, educational and training institutions and banks are crucial to make the target to be achieved in order to get the advantage of the demographic dividend. The challenges before the new skilling process in the new context are complex and difficult as difficult nature of the governance arrangement. Making every stakeholder in the process aware and conscious of the imperative need and the opportunities is the first task. Secondly, bringing a coordinated action among the institutions involved in skilling our youth is the need of the hour. Thirdly, the perception of the stakeholders about vocational education has to be changed. Fourthly, the poor respect and unregulated wage pattern for skilled workers in the unorganized sector turns our youth towards liberal education and hence the problem has to be addressed effectively. Fifthly, the low capacity of the existing institutional arrangements in skilling youth needs collaborative institutional arrangements to

Table 6.1: Incremental Skill Gap across Various Industries in India in 2022

Industry	*Incremental requirement (in millions)*
Building and Construction Industry	33.0
Infrastructure Sector	103.1
Real Estate Services	14.0
Gems and Jewellery	4.6
Leather and Leather Goods	4.6
Organized Retail	17.3
Textiles and Clothing	26.2
Electronics and IT Hardware	3.3
Auto and Auto Components	35.0
IT and ITES	5.3
Banking, Financial Services and Insurance	4.2
Furniture and Furnishings	3.4
Tourism and Hospitality Services	3.6
Construction Material and Building Hardware	1.4
Chemicals and Pharmaceuticals	1.9
Food Processing	9.3
Healthcare	12.7
Transportation and Logistics	17.7
Media and Entertainment	3.0
Education and Skill Development Services	5.8
Select Informal Employment Sectors (Domestic Help, Beauticians, Security Guards)	37.6
Incremental Total	**347**

Sources: IMaCS reports "Human Resource and Skill Gap Requirements (2022)", 2008; Aon Hewitt report "Talent Projections and Skill Gap Analysis for the Infrastructure Sector (2022)", 2011, National Skill Development Corporation (NSDC). Cited from Dilip Chenoy's chapter Skill Development in India: A Transformation in the Making.

increase the efficiency and effectiveness in skilling youth. Finally, people perception about professionalization of tasks and works in everyday life has to be created. Against the above background, the new exercises of skilling has to take place. Estimates have been made as to how much workforce needed to India skill-wise in the coming years.

A Micro Analysis

In this context, a small exercise has been done in a centrally funded deemed university (Gandhigram Rural Institute—Deemed University). Students who are pursuing social science stream are drawn from departments for interaction. Almost all the students are first generation students from their families to pursue higher education. All are stipend holders belonging to socially deprived communities. But they are above average students in terms of their studies. Before initiating the discussion a detailed briefing was done about the context, new opportunities, new policy and the initiatives to be taken.

First their aspiration was taken up for discussion. Many respondents informed that they come to studies in social science stream not out of passion. Their financial condition did not permit them to join in technical programmes in engineering colleges and hence they have joined the social science programmes. They informed in the discussion that there is a wide prevalent view among the people that technical education gives job opportunities with high salaries. In every village one could see the impact of technical education in many of the families. People picked up the perception from seeing the reality. Of course liberal education also provided such job opportunities, but not to level of technical education. Their immediate concern is to get an employment opportunity. Their focus is to pass service commission examination and get some jobs in the government. Many of them told that they are planning to write group examination. They are post-graduate students and yet beyond the clerical post they could not fix their goal. When they are drawn towards skill development issues in the discussion they openly admitted that they are in paper and they could not see anything tangible in the campus barring a few skill oriented certificate courses. They are also output oriented and not outcome oriented. In the evening a few certificate courses and diploma courses are being offered. Many of the students believe that they are additional qualifications. But in reality they have not increased the saleability of the students. The students argued that skill related courses should be given by those who are in trade on the skill. Hence, they argued that in every Arts and Science College and in every general university, skill giving technical institutions have to be started. When the skill gap was discussed with them, they started arguing that the university system is not addressing the needs of neither the society, nor the industry nor the students. Every segment is working in isolation. The students have informed that many of the teachers working in higher learning institutions are not able to inform the students about the current position of the labour market. Because the teachers have not equipped themselves with the current status of affairs.

But everyone of the participants has indicated that they have a few skills, but they are not market oriented. They acquired the skills through informal training which are need-based. Further some of the participants informed that they acquired it through their parents. It was interesting to note that with the available skill they earn money while they are doing programme in the higher education institution. Table 6.2 explains the students earning capacity by using their skills acquired through informal training and from their parents. But to win over poverty they earn money and spend for their education. They made it very clear that they want to learn more skills, but there is no institutional mechanism available within the college and university system to acquire skills.

Further they argued, if facilities are available in the university system, they can acquire more sophisticated skills formally to the national and international standard. The students have posited certain questions and of which one is

Table 6.2: Earn While You Learn

Sl. No.	Nature of Work	Average Earning Per Day	Average Days Per Month	Per Month Earning
1.	Helper to electricians	350	6 days	2100
2.	Waiter in catering	450	5 days	2250
3.	Mason	600	6 days	3600
4.	Kitchen assistant	350	6 days	2100
5.	Gardener	250	4 days	1000
6.	Night watchman	200	8 days	1600
7.	Toilet cleaner	300	6 days	1800
8.	Helper to mason	250	6 days	1500
9.	Helper to carpenter	250	6 days	1500
10.	Call driver	600	4 days	2400
11.	Painting	500	4 days	2000

Source: Computed.

very important. Why university system has not contextualized in terms of integrating vocational education and training system with liberal education offered in the university system? Despite policy pronouncements, resource allocation why higher learning institutions have not acted fastly to make of the new opportunities?

There are a few skills which are being offered in the university system do not reflect the quality standard. In order to increase the saleability of the students, their skill level has to be enhanced. The students in the arts and social science branches are having a clear cut demand. What they demanded is the academic programmes have to be conducted in the morning hours from 9 a.m. to 1.30 p.m. Afternoon from 2.30 p.m. to 7.30 p.m. students will be given option to go for vocational education. The university system either has to create a community college or it should have tie up with industrial training centres or polytechnic colleges. An undergraduate student can get at least a few skills which are in demand in the market. Focus could be given on the skills which are required for unorganized sectors.

What is the immediate requirement in arts and science colleges is the next question on which interaction took place. Students need awareness about social entrepreneurship and for which every college and every university should have a centre for entrepreneurship. Students should be motivated to acquire a few skills and for which centre for skill development or community college has to be created in every university and every college. Otherwise a meaningful MoU has to be signed between a polytechnic and the college for acquiring a skill sets. Market oriented skills have to be offered in the community colleges. In order to enable the students to acquire skill sets, the main programme has to be conducted in the morning hours and skills have to be offered in the evening. The skills needed for them are shown in Table 6.3.

Table 6.3: Needed Skills Set as per the Demand of the Students

Sl. No.	*Skills Needed*	*Sl. No.*	*Skills Needed*
1.	Car Driving	17.	Gardening
2.	Truck Driving	18.	Communication
3.	Earth Mover Driving	19.	Secretarial assistance
4.	AC Mechanic	20.	Statistical analysis
5.	Compounder in Hospital	21.	Report writing for newspapers
6.	Computing	22.	Natural beautification
7.	Nursing	23.	Artificial beautification
8.	Old Age Care	24.	Hair clipping
9.	Event Management	25.	Sales and service
10.	Plumbing	26.	Cell phone repairing
11.	Electrician	27.	Photography
12.	Fitter	28.	Legal assistance
13.	Turner	29.	Masonry
14.	Hospitality	30.	Accounting
15.	Catering	31.	Painting
16.	Carpentry		

Source: Computed.

The above skills are projected by the students based on their own cursory analysis and understanding of the labour market. While interacting with them, they informed that they need more of counselling rather than teaching from their teachers. Teachers guidance will help them to move in their career ladder.

Table 6.4: Demand for Soft Skills by the Students

Sl. No.	*Skills Needed*
1.	Personality Development
2.	Communication skill
3.	Presentation skill
4.	Leadership skill
5.	Career Planning skill
6.	Problem Solving skills
7.	Contact Resolution skills
8.	Critical Thinking skills
9.	Mentoring skills
10.	Public Speaking skill
11.	Development Reporting skill
12.	Proposal Writing skill

Source: Computed.

The skills they acquire should be certified by the sector council for increasing their employability instead of issuing certificate in the university itself. National employment portal has to be created and the available skill force coming out from the colleges have to be put in the portal and thus the employers are facilitated to look for candidates and come to colleges for recruitment. In such a way the higher learning institutions have to be reoriented and repositioned.

Integrated Analysis

It is an obvious fact that proliferation of engineering colleges in higher education in India reveals that the skilled human power production has gone unexpectedly on the higher side. Apparently it is true. Even then only 20 per cent of the students coming out from the technical institutions are having the needed skills to suit the requirements of the industries and service sectors. There is yet another reality that in higher education system still 56 per cent of the students are from the Arts and Science stream. It is a paradox that when the quantum of enrollment rate increases in higher learning institutions, sharply the labour market faces shortage of skilled human power. It reflects the reality of skill gap. It is to be admitted that the institutions have not produced skilled students needed to the market requirements. At the same time students aspiration level is high to acquire skills needed to the market. But the facilities and schemes available in the arts and science colleges and general universities are inadequate to meet the requirements of either the students or the market. Students have projected certain categorical demands through their interaction. They are:

(a) Arts and Science colleges have to run academic programmes from morning 9.00 to 1.30 noon everyday and they are to be allowed to undergo skill training in the evening to make the students employable.
(b) Every arts and science college and general university should have community college which should train students in skills. The community colleges have to offer skills which are required to labour market.
(c) In the absence of community colleges MoU has to be signed with nearly ITI or Polytechnics and by which the students from the arts and science colleges have to be trained in skills.
(d) A common web portal has to be created to put the names of qualified students in terms of skills to meet the market needs.
(e) The certification process has to be changed from the existing practices to skill sector council certification.
(f) Higher learning institutions have to be oriented to change the mode of transaction from output to outcome.
(g) Like the Western countries, wage rates have to be fixed for skilled works and thereby we can make the society to recognize the skilled workers value.

Table 6.5: State-wise Distribution of India's Technical Training Institutions

States/Union Territories	*Arts, Science & Commerce*	*ENGG, Tech.*	*Medical Colleges*	*Teacher training Colleges*	*Polytechnics*	*Others*	*Total*
Andhra Pradesh	1,603	278	311	343	140	93	2768
Arunachal Pradesh	10	1	1	2	1	1	16
Assam	348	4	10	40	9	28	439
Bihar	800	10	28	15	12	36	901
Chhattisgarn	334	16	20	4	10	51	435
Goa	23	5	7	2	5	7	49
Gujarat	518	45	90	125	73	283	1,134
Haryana	168	45	35	37	34	18	337
Himachal Pradesh	95	6	12	30	6	29	178
Jammu & Kashmir	65	5	6	127	12	19	234
Jharkhand	113	11	7	8	8	23	170
Karnataka	930	134	423	68	179	146	1,880
Kerala	189	99	125	21	56	82	572
Madhya Pradesh	712	74	97	21	44	147	1,095
Maharashtra	1,018	193	345	255	194	414	2,419
Manipur	58	1	1	6	1	4	71
Meghalaya	54	1	0	3	1	3	62
Mizoram	26	1	0	2	2	1	32
Nagaland	41	0	0	4	2	22	69
Orissa	702	45	58	13	31	92	941
Punjab	232	53	61	47	18	49	460
Rajasthan	751	50	34	111	17	113	1,076
Sikkim	3	1	2	2	2	1	11
Tamil Nadu	693	269	198	160	209	116	1645
Tripura	14	2	3	1	2	6	28
Uttar Pradesh	1,637	114	93	121	107	702	2,774
Uttarakhand	87	12	20	1	24	28	172
West Bengal	374	60	68	66	40	35	643
A&N Islands	3	0	0	1	2	1	7
Chandigarh	12	7	4	3	1	1	28
Dadra	0	0	0	0	1	0	1
Daman & Diu	1	0	0	1	1	0	3
Delhi	68	20	24	10	23	64	209
Lakshadweep	0	0	0	0	0	0	0
Puducherry	17	5	9	19	5	4	59
India	**11,699**	**1,567**	**2,092**	**1,669**	**1,272**	**2,619**	**20,918**

Source: Ministry of Human Resource Development, Government of India.

Conclusion

First and foremost skill development consciousness has to be created among the people and the students. At present there is inadequate awareness on skill development among the students and the teachers. There is no initiative at the institutional level for skilling the students' youth. This has to be addressed immediately. Secondly, all the arts and science colleges have to have community colleges and otherwise the colleges have to sign MoU with the industrial technical institutions and polytechnic colleges. This kind of initiative will help the students of Arts and Science colleges to acquire skills needed to the market from the ITI and Polytechnic institutions. Private institutions which are having both technical and Arts and Science colleges should adopt a flexible arrangement of allowing students to move from Arts and Science colleges to technical institutions to acquire skill. Thirdly, students have to be prepared to acquire a skill set to increase their employability. Fourthly, the working hours of the colleges have to be changed. In Arts and Science colleges office hours have to be fixed between 9.00 and 1.30 noon. Afternoon students have to be allowed to go for skilling. A new awakening has to be created among the students that adding skills will benefit them to increase their employability. Fifthly, standardization of skills have to be done and in the same way certification process has to be done meticulously to increase rigour in certification. Sixthly, National Employment portal has to be created for the visibility of available workforce on different skills to enable the employer to locate the workforce needed to them. Seventhly, wages have to be standardized with an objective of removing stigma on the labourers. Eight, needed system has to be created for the workforce who are working in unorganized sector to protect their interest. All the works have to be carried out in a war footing by integrating all the agencies involved in skill development in India.

Notes

1. Targets subject to discussions based on inputs received from the Ministry.
2. Target set for RSETIs MoRD as 3,00,000. As per the Quarterly report it is mentioned as 2,92,050. Need to resolve this with the Ministry.
3. Ministries have not reported the data.

4. Target set for the D/o Electronics and Information Technology for 2013-14 as 5,00,000. As per the Quarterly report it is revised as 5,10,000.
5. Target was revised downwards from 6 lakhs to 4 lakhs by the Ministry.
6. Target set for Ministry as 1,50,000. As per the Quarterly report figures it is 92,648. Need to resolve it with the Ministry.
7. G. Palanithurai, 2012, *Social Relevance of Higher Learning Institutions*, New Delhi: Concept Publishing Company Pvt. Ltd., pp. 99-121.
8. Amit Endu Palit, 2009, "Skills Development in India: Challenges and Strategies", *ISAS Working Paper*, National University of Singapore No. 89, September.

References

1. Ministry of Labour and Employment, 2012, *National Policy on Skill Development 2009*, New Delhi: Government of India.
2. Prime Minister's National Council for Skill Development was established to coordinate and supervise the entire activities of skill development in the country. There is yet another board called National Skill Development Coordination Board which was established to coordinate the activities of seventeen Ministries and the private sector initiatives through National Skill Development Corporation.
3. National Vocational Education Qualification Framework (NVEQF) was evolved and it is in place at present.
4. National Skill Development Fund has been set-up and it has got 25 billion rupees in the corpus.
5. 500 million workforces have to be trained through institutions and of them 350 million have to be trained by the 17 Ministries and 150 million to be trained by the private sector initiatives through NSDC.
6. Skill Development Progress (FY 2013-14)
   A total target of skilling 72.82 lakhs was accepted by various Central Government Ministries, and the NSDC, for the year 2013-14. The table below shows the allocated targets, and the latest status of target achievements as reported by these organizations to the National Skill Development Agency:

7

Village Placement Programme

An Enabler to Learn about Communities

Introduction

It is a well-known fact that in India the Higher Learning Institutions never involve themselves in outreach activities in a big way as they perform the other two functions namely teaching and research. If the performance of teachers in higher learning institutions is evaluated in terms of their output in research and teaching, barring a few premier institutions, other higher learning institutions concentrate more on teaching and they do research occasionally that too for career building.[1] In this context giving importance to outreach programme is something unusual in the higher learning institutions. Of course, through National Social Service Programme (NSS) students are reaching the communities for a few days which was considered as base for outreach activities of the academic institutions in India. Beyond that, systematic and scientific way of outreach programmes is rare in the Higher Learning Institutions in India. Yet a few institutions are involved in outreach programmes and of which Gandhigram Rural Institute – Deemed University is one, a fully Centrally funded Institute. The Gandhigram Rural Institute was one among fourteen institutions started in India at the dawn of Independence based on Dr. Radhakrishnan Committee Report.[2] Rural Institute was organized as a distinct category of higher learning institution to work for rural transformation through working with rustic folk in the rural areas. Of the fourteen, thirteen institutions have disappeared from scene and the Gandhigram Rural Institute is one remaining as distinct institute meant for the same old objectives and values.[3] It has got six decades experience in working with the communities. Yet, it could not make any significant impact in the higher learning institutions in terms of outreach programmes on the direction it envisaged. If the higher learning institutions both universities and colleges in India are involved in outreach activities in a systematic way, a number of socio-economic problems could be tackled directly by the higher learning institutions. Such potentials are available with the higher learning institutions.[4] It is unfortunate that our policy-makers and funding institutions have not taken serious initiatives to strengthen the extension dimension of the higher learning institutions as they concentrate on the two others namely teaching and research. In order to demonstrate the huge potential of the outreach activities, the present chapter is written based on the personal experience involved in outreach programme of Political Science Department in the name of Village Placement Programme (VPP). It is one among the outreach activities of the Gandhigram Rural Institute.[5]

Difficulties before us

Even in the Gandhigram Rural Institute it is not so easy for us to convince both the faculty and the students to go to villages and work with people at least for the sake of students and teachers if not for the sake of communities. Because both students and teachers have to work in the field in the name of outreach programme without theoretical input. The main weakness we have identified is lack of theoretical rigour in our extension activities. Since, the Gandhigram Rural Institute is a designated extension oriented institute which is compelling the students and teachers to carry out the extension activities. Moreover, it is a Gandhian Rural Institute, a special status of Deemed University has been granted to the Gandhigram Rural

Institute. We made it a mandate to keep some of the activities to show that we are fulfilling the basic objectives of the institute. Further, the expectations of the recruitment agencies who recruit our students for jobs expect that our students should have more grip on the field along with theory. Faculties are interested in following the traditional universities and not interested in making the traditional universities to follow the Gandhigram Rural Institute in carrying out outreach programme. Obviously, there are two reasons for the above stand. One is that there is no theoretical argument built on extension over a period of time based on their experience to convince the traditional university teachers to follow the extension activities. To build career of academics in rural institute's faculty traditional university system will be much easier and hence, they try to move into the track of the traditional universities.

Of course, there are problems in organizing outreach programmes in the rural areas in an integrated way. In 1950s and 1960s, organizing outreach programme was easy as the communities were in need of many services from the outside agencies as Government's interventions in the villages were very less. Further, teachers went with only ten to twenty students. It was useful both to the community and to the students. Now, the Government has more number of development schemes. In Tamil Nadu alone three hundred and sixty nine development schemes including ninety schemes of the Central Government. In this context one has to think what can be delivered in the villages to the communities. Further, students are admitted in large numbers in all the programmes as per the stipulation of the Central Government to increase the enrollment rate and hence teachers find it difficult to take all the students to villages and stay in the villages and work with the people meaningfully for the benefit of both. Finding places for accommodation with facilities minimum to the level of the expectations of the students and more particularly to find out works for the students in the villages. Moreover, in the absence of clarity on the part of the faculty in terms of approach and tools to be used in the villages in the backdrop of the theories, working with the people in the villages are equal to Rural Development Tourism.

Approaches, tools and strategies adopted in 1950s are of no use at present as development of the rural areas is in the hands of the Government through plethora of rural development schemes and programmes. Unless universities development new perspectives evolve new tools and strategies extension becomes a ritual. By projecting the above arguments, the teachers are reluctant to undertake this programme. But it is a mandated one in the system. The teachers instead of attempting to develop new perspectives and tools, they project logistic problems as barriers to conduct outreach programmes. Keeping large number of students in the villages both boys and girls for seven days by giving works to them and providing needed facilities to them are real logistics problems for the teachers. Since, it is an expenditure borne by the university the cost worked out to Rs. 65 per day by the institute per head really put the teachers in tough task. In the backdrop of all the difficulties, the teachers and students are in the villages and perform certain tasks which are beneficial to the communities and to the students. The institute has constituted many committees to revamp the programme and to suggest ways and means to improve and innovate. Nothing came out from the committees.[6]

A Programme under Analysis

Village Placement Programme is one of the few activities designed by the Gandhigram Rural Institute under outreach programme activities and the same is for a period of seven days. Apart from the above, there are a number of activities carried out for the benefit of the villages both in villages and in the campus by bringing the actual stakeholders from the rural areas. Students and teachers are involved in all these activities according to their convenience in different periods. Every student in the University has to stay in villages for a period of seven days every year as per the mandate of the VPP system. It is an approved mandated academic activity and no one is excluded from this programme. Both teachers and students should be in the programme. The date for Village Placement Programme will be fixed and notified in the university calendar itself. in 2012, it was fixed from 13th to 19th August, 2012 for Humanities and Social Science. Place has to be selected by the faculty and activities have to be evolved by the faculty and students through an interactive process. Logistics will be supported by the University. This write up will make an analysis of the VPP carried out in a village by the Department of Political Science and Development Administration.

A Case Study

For our analysis the Department of Political Science and Development Administration has been taken since the author is part of the process and intensively attached with the programme. Every year one faculty member from the department has to coordinate the entire programme and all other faculty members participate in the programme. This year Dr. Sonkhogin Haokip, Assistant Professor is the coordinator for the Programme. He is from Manipur and he is new to this place. Yet he has taken up the responsibility of organizing the same as mandated by the university. He has to get funds from the university and submit accounts for the same. Totally he is responsible and accountable for the entire programme. All other faculty members will facilitate and cooperate with the coordinator for organizing the VPP. He in fact well in advance organized the students and formed the students into eight groups. These eight groups are meant for carrying out learning activities in the village. From among the students, a few committees have been formed to manage the programme effectively by themselves in extending logistic support to the programme in the village. Once group formation was over, Prof. G. Palanithurai has been given the responsibility of giving orientation to the students on Village Placement Programme (VPP).

Orientation to the Students

On 10th of August, 2012 half a day was allotted for orientation programme. It was done for the whole department students. All the teachers were in the orientation programme. Prof. G. Palanithurai explained the theoretical assumptions of the outreach or extension programme. Higher learning institutions have knowledge skill, technology, resources and capacity and the above can be extended directly to the communities. By extending the above to the communities, lot of benefits the communities can get directly from the institute and by which the communities can develop themselves. Further by doing the extension activities in the community's students will enhance their skill and capacity. By performing the above task continuously through a systematic way both teachers and the students will be sensitive on the issues of the people. Their values, commitment and social responsibility will be enhanced. He outlined how effectively the programme can be conceived with active involvement of teachers and the students through interaction. He effectively explained how the programme could be made learner centric. And equally he explained how effectively the outreach activities planned by the students and faculties can be carried out in the villages with the active involvement of the community representatives and students. He further succinctly elaborated the benefits the learners get out of the programme. He outlined the parameters with which programme has to be evaluated. He listed out the activities to be carried out in the villages by the students when they stay in the villages.[7] By this process of orientation every student was clear about why they are visiting and staying in villages. Later they chalked out the programme tentatively for all the seven days. They collected needed material for academic works and implements for physical works from NSS unit.

Background of the Department

Here, it is to be noted that the Department of Political Science is under UGC – SAP, DRS-1 on 'Local Governance.' Further, the

Department has got a M.A. Innovative Programme approved by the UGC on Governance and Development. Apart from the above, the Department has got a unique M.A. Programme. It is a five year Integrated Programme on Development Administration. So, totally 109 students are in the Political Science Department. In the whole of South India in terms of student strength it is the biggest Department. The Department has got Rajiv Gandhi Chair for Panchayati Raj Studies with separate building for training activities. The Rajiv Gandhi Chair has got enormous materials on Panchayati Raj for awareness creation and training Panchayat functionaries. All the project staff is well trained and oriented as master trainers to conduct training programme. They have the capability to train Panchayat leaders. There are two Professors, two Associate Professors and two Assistant Professors in the Department. The Department has two M.A. Programmes, M. Phil. Programme and Ph.D. Programme. The department has been specializing in governance at grassroots. All the teachers are in the same field with the different areas of specialization. Our Ph.D. programme is focusing on grassroots governance and transformative process of the communities. The Department has got a departmental library with 2,500 current titles relevant to students and faculty, a Mini Seminar hall with all state of the art facilities, a smart classroom, a computer centre with 20 systems for students with internet connections. All the teachers are provided with one system and one laptop. In such a way Department is equipped. The whole Department is fully equipped through the project activities. Enormous resources are available for the students and teachers. Many of the students are having their personal computers.[8]

Village Selection

Since, villages for VPP have to be selected by the Coordinator of the programme, Karisalpatti Gram Panchayat has been selected based on a few criteria. Availability of space for the students to stay, cooperation of the Panchayat functionaries and civil societies, water availability, availability of sanitation facilities, space for academic work and availability of food at an affordable cost are the criteria with which village is being selected. With the above criteria, the Karisalpatti Gram Panchayat was selected by the coordinator. Karisalpatti Gram Panchayat is a multi-caste village Panchayat. Fairly a big village and the Panchayat has got awards for two times and for which Gandhigram played a significant role in building the capacity of Panchayat leaders. Further, the Panchayat is free from intense social conflicts. Panchayat has got a community hall, good toilet facilities, and one small library in the Panchayat building. Since, the community felt that they are also going to get some benefits out of camps of the university students the entire village communities positively worked for the camp and helped the students. Panchayat leader took major responsibilities for extending logistics support. Previously, for the Panchayat our student extended help for micro-plan preparation by collecting data from the villages and conducting PRA exercises. Moreover, a toilet facility was created long back very near to the community hall through a project of our department. Hence, a positive response comes from this village for village placement programme. A few published studies on the same Gram Panchayat are also available and that will also help the students to relook at the villages now. This Gram Panchayat is in Reddiarchatram Block in Dindigul District. It is thirty kilometers away from the university.

Group Discussion

Eight groups have been formed already among the students for the village placement programme. After the orientation programme they have started the group discussion to finalize the activities to be done in the village. They have decided that each group should have students from all the classes from first year to final year. Each group should be led by one student who should be sociable and communicative. He or she should be able to write the report based on the input given by every member in the group. Group leader should have grip over English language and at the same time he or she should be more democratic to listen and respect others, views. In each group women students and students from marginalized communities should be made members. While giving group leadership consideration should be given for gender and details.

By following such norms on a consensus basis they have chosen the group leaders. Group leader has to brief all the members about the tasks to be performed everyday and he or she has to write the report based on the group discussion after visiting the field to collect data. The leader has to present the report in the review meeting everyday evening with the above understanding groups have been firmed up. They are in eight groups. Apart from the above groups they formed six logistic committees. They are mess committee, cultural programme committee, general discipline committee and reception committee. The above committees will help the coordinator to run the programme smoothly. It has been designed in such a way that the whole programme has to be designed and managed by the students themselves. Co-coordinator of the programme will be only facilitator.

Table 7.1: Seven Days Activities: Activity Schedule of Village Placement Programme (13.08.2012 – 19.08.2012)

13.08.2012

Time	*Activities*
9.40 – 10.40	Travel to Karisalpatti Village
10.45 – 12.00	Cleaning the Community Hall for their stay
12.00 – 13.00	Chalking the activities for the day
13.00 – 14.00	Lunch Break
14.00 – 15.00	Rest
15.00 – 18.00	Transact Walk – Resource Identification
18.00 – 19.00	Tea Break
19.00 – 20.30	Group Discussion on the works done in the field
20.30 – 21.30	Dinner
21.30 – 22.00	Cultural Programme for and among the students
22.30 – 23.00	Wrap-up and Review

14.08.2012

Time	*Activities*
5.00 – 6.00	Getting up from Bed and doing Routine exercises
6.00 – 7.00	Inter-religious Prayer and Meeting
7.00 – 7.30	Tea
7.30 – 8.30	Group Discussion on the works done in the field
8.30 – 9.30	Breakfast
9.30 – 12.30	Organizing Awareness programme on Gram Sabha in the village with the Panchayat President
12.30 – 13.00	Review on the Awareness Programme
13.00 – 14.00	Lunch Break
14.00 – 14.30	Group deliberation for fieldwork
14.30 – 18.00	Groups -- Separately going to field
18.00 – 19.00	Reaching the camp site and Rest
19.00 – 20.00	Group discussion on the data collected from the field
20.00 – 21.00	Dinner
21.00 – 22.00	Writing reports by respective groups
22.00 PM	Wrap-up Review

15.08.2012

Time	*Activities*
5.00 – 6.00	Wake up and Routine exercises
6.00 – 7.00	Prayer
7.00 – 7.30	Preparatory work for Independence Day celebration in Panchayat Office
7.30 – 8.30	Breakfast
8.45 – 10.30	Flag hoisting programme.
10.30 – 13.00	Attending Gram Sabha meeting as observer
13.00 – 14.00	Lunch break
14.00 – 15.00	Rest
15.00 – 18.00	Fieldwork
18.00 – 19.00	Tea break
19.00 – 20.00	Review meeting
20.00 – 21.00	Dinner
21.00 – 22.00	Report writing
22.00 PM	Wrap-up

16.08.2012

Time	*Activities*
5.00 AM	Wake up and Routine exercises
6.00 AM	Prayer
7.00 AM	Tea
7.30 AM	Group Discussion
8.30 AM	Breakfast
9.30 AM	Field visit
13.00 PM	Lunch Break
15.00 PM	Field visit
18.00 PM	Review Meeting
20.00 PM	Dinner
21.00 PM	Report Writing
22.00 PM	Wrap-up

17.08.2012

Time	*Activities*
5.00 AM	Wake up and Routine exercises
6.00 AM	Prayer
7.00 AM	Tea
7.30 AM	Group discussion on the report
8.30 AM	Breakfast
9.30 AM	Mobilization of farmers for KVK activities
13.00 PM	Lunch break
14.00 PM	Review meeting
15.00 PM	Field visit
16.30 PM	Tea break
17.00 PM	Report writing
20.00 PM	Dinner
21.00 PM	Review meeting
22.00 PM	Wrap-up

18.08.2012

Time	*Activities*
5.00 AM	Wake up and Routine exercises
6.00 AM	Prayer
7.00 AM	Tea
7.30 AM	Group discussion
8.30 AM	Breakfast
9.30 AM	A few groups visited the field to fill the gap in the fieldwork and other groups involved in report writing
13.00 PM	Lunch break
14.00 PM	Review meeting
15.00 PM	Group presentation
17.30 PM	Evaluation and observation
19.00 PM	Review of the report based on observations
20.00 PM	Dinner
21.00 PM	Group discussion for way forward
22.00 PM	Wrap-up

19.08.2012

Time	*Activities*
5.00 AM	Wake up and Routine exercises
6.00 AM	Prayer
7.00 AM	Tea
7.30 AM	Evaluation of the programme
8.30 AM	Breakfast
10.00 AM	Departure to Campus

Learning Methodology

Students have evolved different methods to elicit response from the villagers. They keep the check-list with them and initiate a dialogue with the respondents. It is not an interview, but it is only a dialogue. They select opinion-makers in the villages and interact with them. They develop stories out of it. For certain issue they conduct face-to-face interview with interview schedule. There are certain issues which require direct observation. To check whether water supply is on time, whether schools run in time, whether teachers are in time, whether blackboards are in the classrooms and the like are being observed personally by the students by themselves. Even for face-to-face interview they first select the individual and ask them their convenient place and time accordingly they conduct dialogues with them. Focus group discussion they have conducted. Report card method has been used to assess the level of satisfaction among the people about the services delivered by the Government institutions. To study the transformatory process case study method has been followed. Even in case study method, they used different strategies. A number of nuances they have adopted. They are to be properly explained in proper terms.

Reporting

The first group which took responsibility to study the impact of MGNREGA has adopted case study method and wrote stories about twenty nine women from the *Dalit* community. The thirteen members under the coordination of the group leader Ms. M. Midhila had an extensive interaction with the women workers on different issues. They came with a set of observation based on their interview with the MGNREGA women. First and foremost is the wage parity between men and women was achieved through this scheme. From their perspective, it is a revolutionary scheme. All the cases have demonstrated that their life has been changed because of the scheme. They felt that they are not working under private individual. They had a feeling that they are working in the Government. Because of the pay parity we are empowered to demand wage parity while going to work in the farm land. The amount earned through this scheme is being spent for children's education and health apart from purchasing a few household articles. Some of them have savings. Since, they are members of self-help groups (SHGs), this savings have been used in the group money. They purchased gold studs for their daughters which they never dreamt in their life. Many of the women said that their husbands are not coming to this scheme. They are going for farm work as their wage is very high. The wage of the farm workers has been increased because of MGNREGA. Students felt that enormous scope and potentials are in the scheme and they can be documented scientifically. The students have suggested that with the help of the university students throughout India case studies can be conducted to analyze transformative process in the rural rustic folk through this scheme.[9]

The second group under the leadership of Gokul Govind R. has had taken the task of studying the general trend of people participation in the process of governance and development. For cultural and social activities people participate effectively. Even for political party meeting party men participate and beyond that people do not participate in common development activities in an organized way. Self-help group members participate in group meetings as they deal with credits. Beyond that for the development of the Panchayat there is no such strong participation. Students argued that there is no participatory culture among the people in the rural areas. Students argue that this issue has to be seen in the backdrop of theory on participation.[10]

The third group under the leadership of Thamaraikkannan has conducted an in-depth study about the empowerment process of self-help group women. The SHG members are working hard in the group with determination and aspiration. Almost all the poor women are organized and enrolled as members. One could see the visible transformation among the women in terms of their attitudes and behaviour. It gives a sense that a revolution is taking place in the villages silently. Absolutely there is no money lending by the external agency in this village. Because huge money transactions are taking place among themselves. The women are articulate, socially conscious as they are trained and oriented. But they are apolitical. Their awareness level is very high. All the scheme details are obtained by them. Their periodical visits to urban areas, banks, Government offices and attending orientation programme have empowered them. But their work load has been increased both in the house and in the group. Since, they handle money and find source of income their level of happiness is very high. Further, MGNREGA has further increased the money transactions of the poor women. One could see the level of empowerment of women through normative standard.[11]

The fourth group under the leadership of Lakshmanan, C. dealt with the accountability. By their interaction they came to a conclusion that there is no awareness about the public accountability. Everyone in public institution feels that they are answerable to their superior officials in the same administrative set-up. They have no sense of accountability to the real masters. Real masters are the people. The whole accountability system is built upward and not downwards to the people. Social audit and mechanisms are very much needed but they are not in operation. Awareness is needed on this aspect among the people.[12]

The fifth group under the leadership of Appu, T.N. has studied the functioning of *Gram Sabha*. Since, they were in the villages during *Gram Sabha* meeting period, they have attended the *Gram Sabha* meeting as observes with the permission of the *Panchayat* president. The whole process has been observed by the students. They also participated in the *Gram Sabha* mobilization along with *panchayats*. From their observation it is found that the *Gram Panchayat* has not taken enough steps as stipulated in the guidelines to mobilize people for *Gram Sabha*. Secondly, only a few attended the *Gram Sabha* meeting. Even ward members have not attended. But within a few hours signatures have been obtained from the people for submission to the Collector Office. Why this poor show in *Gram Sabha* has been analyzed. Students have interacted with Village *Panchayat* President, Ward Members and *Gram Sabha* members on subsequent days. It was a serious discussion. They found out that people feel that it is only a place where *Gram Panchayat* president collects petition and there is no response for the petitions. Further, whatever is being decided, has not been carried out. There is no meaningful discussion in the *Gram Sabha*. *Panchayat* leaders do not want to take the people into confidence and hence they are not taking earnest effort to convene the meeting. People feel that it is a waste of time. Even the people who participated in the *Gram Sabha* meeting are SHG members that too from beneficiaries of MGNREGA. Even in discussion people are not discussing their problems and they are asked to speak on the subjects given by the State Government. It is considered as ritual. While looking at participation, it is found that traditional *Panchayat* leader has been given time and he spoke at length in *Gram Sabha* meeting. Absolutely quorum is not maintained. *Panchayat* leader said that as all the needs of the people are fulfilled and there is no necessity for them to attend the *Gram Sabha* meeting. Something is obvious from the interaction of students with different stakeholders of *Gram Sabha* that neither the *Panchayat* leaders nor the people are aware of the potentials of *Gram Sabha*.[13]

The sixth group under the leadership of Ms. Ngachawon Ningchen studied the functioning of *Panchayats* from the perspective of transparency. This aspect has been studied through focus group discussion in different places and interacted with many opinion-makers of the village. They found out that absolutely there is no transparency in the functioning of *Panchayats*. There is a provision in the village *Panchayat* office to display all income and expenditure details. The first *Panchayat* president had developed this practice and it was not followed subsequently. The students checked with the *Panchayat* ward members about the functioning of the *Gram Panchayat*. They also informed the students that they are not aware of many of the details. But they get details from the *Panchayat* secretary. In the discussion with opinion-makers, the students found out that the *Panchayat* president is not transparent, but she is non-corrupt. When there is no transparency in the State Government offices how do they expect transparency from the *Panchayat*. This is the observation of the students.[14]

The seventh group under the leadership of Ms. Mruthusha Achari adopted report card method to elicit the opinion about the service delivery and made personal visits to some of the public institutions. In this village *Panchayat* drinking water supply functioning of PDS and roads are good. The street lights are properly maintained. All the public toilets are being used, but they are not maintained properly. School is functioning, blackboards are in the school, good building facilities are available, but there is no Head Master for the school for the past seven years. Nobody to bother in this village. Because alternatives are available.[15]

The eighth group under the leadership of Sudheesh, N.S. has studied the Traditional Panchayat System in the same village Karisalpatti. Since, it is a multi-caste village, there are four traditional *Panchayats* functioning in the *Panchayat* areas. The students have brought out the whole range of activities carried out by the traditional *Panchayats*. From conducting temple festivals to deliver judgement on criminal complaints the traditional *Panchayats* are performing their duties. Participation of stakeholders is very effective. The whole transaction is transparent and they are accountable to their members. The drawback they have noticed is the absence of women, while comparing the traditional *Panchayats* with Constitutional *Panchayats*. The students have argued that the traditional *Panchayats* are more vibrant than the Constitutional *Panchayats*. The students observed that people feel that the traditional *Panchayats* are their *Panchayats* and Constitutional *Panchayats* are the officials' *Panchayats*.[16]

Students' Participation

For *Gram Sabha* meeting on 14th August, 2012, the students along with *Panchayat* leaders conducted an awareness rally in the villages of Karisalpatti Gram Panchayat. Half a day they went door-to-door canvassing for *Gram Sabha* mobilization. It was reported in *Times of India* newspaper.[17] Later on 17th evening yet another programme was organized for farmers of the village by Gandhigram Rural Institute, KVK (Krishi Vigyan Kendra) and for which the students went to each and every house to mobilize the farmers. Totally one full day they spent for *Gram Sabha* and farmers meet. On 15th August, 2012, they participated in Flag Hoisting function and *Gram Sabha* meeting as observers. On 17th August, 2012 students were involved in farmers, mobilization activities for KVK programme of Gandhigram Rural Institute.

Learning from the VPP for the students

Students have reported that they know different kinds of villages functioning at the grassroots. *Gram Panchayat* is with elected representatives of the people. In the same *Gram Panchayat* areas there are many traditional *Panchayats* functioning more vibrantly than the constitutional *Panchayat*. There is yet another village works. Revenue villages are not conterminous with *Gram Panchayats*. Villages have got different faces. Village is a cultural unit, administrative unit, governance unit, social unit, economic unit and political unit. It functions in different style. Jurisdictions of village activities vary. Villages have got more infrastructure facilities and resources. They have fine roads, transport facilities, ground water supply system, cooperative society, schools, sub-centre of the Health Department, community hall, vetenary centre, public distribution system, electricity connection, many temples and churches. Except the community temples all the facilities and institutions are with Government departments. People have no say and they can only make complaints if they are not functioning properly. People do not have needed awareness about the functioning of the *Panchayats* and equally they are not aware of the functioning of the State and Central Government.

People came to know many of the Government schemes only through middleman schemes only through middleman despite the presence of *Panchayat* and television set in each house. Barring a few people do not have the habit of listening news regularly. People evaluate the Government based on the benefits given through different schemes and programmes to the people. People expect not good governance but they expect only benefits.

It is a general understanding of the people in the village that *Panchayat* are with Government and hence they are not evincing keen interest in attending *Gram Sabha* Meeting. When people attend traditional *Panchayat* meeting regularly, why the some persons are not attending the *Gram Sabha* meeting in traditional *Panchayat* they decide and they act. So, people feel that in traditional *Panchayat* they govern and they participate. In constitutional *Panchayat*, State government governs the people through *Panchayati Raj*. Hence, people feel that it is "their governance not our governance". Further, it is considered as petitions receiving meeting. In such a way they perceived it.

From the whole analysis of their exercises students found out the Government is not able to devolve powers to *Panchayats* to decide on their own on issues which are affecting their life. Commensurate with powers resources have to be given to the *Panchayats* to carry activities which they decide in *Gram Sabha* and *Panchayat* Council. In the absence of the above two, it is only a ritual. *Gram Sabha* will not be attractive. One could notice vibrancy in the functioning of traditional *Panchayats*. They have resources and powers as drawn from the community and hence they decide and carry out. They conduct temple festivals, conduct cultural festivals and resolve dispute from civil to criminal. This is the idea of justice works at the grassroots. While mapping the resources available in the village, it is found that all resources are available very near to the habitats of dominant communities. *Dalits* have been neglected. *Dalits* are in a frustrating mood. *Panchayat* is in the hands of the dominant communities and the *Dalit* representatives have not opened their mouth in the meeting due to fear of communal clash. Village *Panchayat* is not evolving development plan for the village. If they develop development plan *Dalit* component plan could be integrated with it.

MGNREGA has created an impeccable impact on the poor. One striking visible impact is that pay parity or wage parity has been achieved between women and men first time in Indian society at the community level. The women, who have earned money through this scheme, have spent for children education and health. They further spent for purchasing household articles. The pitiable part is that the beneficiaries are not aware how much Central Government gives for this scheme. They feel that it is the State Government scheme. Nearly twenty nine case studies have been conducted among the *Dalit* and poor women beneficiaries of MGNREGA. Each case is a classic case for transformatory process. These materials are very useful tools for teaching. In such a way cases have been written and analyzed. At every level people suspect corruption. But they are unable to provide proof.

In every *Panchayat* Office one computer is available and it can be used profitably by the *Panchayats*. If the *Panchayats* clerk is trained in computer operation, computer can be used for *Panchayat* administration. It could be seen at the ground that there is no professionalism in the service points at the grassroots. Service providers require training to make them as professional to deliver services to the community professionally.

It is learnt that Government spends huge money in the villages not on their demand and priorities. Pervious DMK Government has spent 20 lakh rupees to provide basic amenities to the village *Panchayats* under the scheme called *'Anaithu Grama Anna Marumalarchi Thittam'*. Now, the present AIADMK Government spends ranging from Rs. 30 to Rs. 50 lakh rupees in each *Gram Panchayat* areas for the same purpose under the scheme called *'Thai Thittam'*. For the entire amount activities have been finalized by the officials of the State Government. Major amount is being spent on steel, cement and sand. Of course some of the facilities created out of the scheme are underutilized and unutilized. Remarkable changes are taking place among the poor women as they are organized under Self-Help Group. Though they are involved in credit activities, their mobilization and interaction have changed their perceptions and thereby their attitude. In every *Gram Panchayat,* a small library is maintained and there is no reader. Occasionally, it is opened and a very few are coming. But good books are available in the library. Many facilities are created in the villages. But there is no resource allocation for maintenance of all those facilities created through schemes. There are temples of the communities in the villages. Temples are for each caste group. Temple festivals are conducted in the village and for which they mobilize funds from the people. Huge money has been mobilized for temple festivals. The temple committees save money and lend it for the caste members. Absolutely, there is no corruption. The whole transaction has been made in a transparent way.

Here one important issue is noticed. People make allegations against Government systems, but they said that traditional *Panchayats* are honest, temple communities are honest, when they are asked to explain. People said that everyone knows in the villages wherefrom money comes and where it goes whereas nobody knows wherefrom money comes to grassroots from the State and Central Government and how they are spent and for whom they spent and when they spent are not known to people. Poor could not understand the complex governance process. Middlemen are issuing this opportunity to help the poor and get money.

Learning for the Teachers

"As a teacher and Camp In-charge, I have learnt a lot from this camp. First, the sincerity, punctuality, good manners and obedience of the students in this camp have made me really humbled. This camp is by far, the best that I have ever supervised. Secondly, the unconventional methods adopted by the students in collecting data from the villagers who tend to be more effective than the conventional methods applied in social science research has offered tremendous insights into the world of research. Sometimes, I felt as if I have been pushing the students too hard in this camp, but eventually, it pays. Each of the eight groups came out with wonderful reports. I have learnt a lot about Karisalpatti Village from them—how the Village *Panchayat* is functioning, the role of traditional *Panchayats* in influencing people's lives, role of SHGs in empowering women economically and socially, the types of services delivered to the people, people's participation in the affairs of the *Panchayat* including the *Gram Sabha,* functioning of temple committees, youth clubs, and the impact of MGNREGA. Finally, the professionalism of the students in preparing a proposed map of the village where the camp was organized and in interpreting the data and finally in preparing the final reports is really a learning experience for me as a teacher."[18]

Evaluation and Analysis

Students' performance has been evaluated mostly through a normative scale. Their deep involvement in the work and participating in the programme in both academic and logistic activities. How they exhibit their leadership? How they write report, and how they discuss in the group and present the same in the review meeting have been evaluated. Above all how they maintain discipline in the programme? is also considered. Have they participated in the programme with an interest and with a sense of commitment have been seen? By using the entire parameters student's performance has been evaluated. Based on the above criteria, five students have been selected for giving certificate of merit.

Conclusion

From the whole programme both the teachers and students of the Department of Political Science and Development Administration have learnt many lessons akin to their subject. Many of the gaps between theory and practice have been identified only during the VPP in Karisalpatti Village Panchayat. Teachers found many new issues for investigation. Students who confronted issues while they were in the classrooms found answer for their problems. Students have got deep insights into the issues of local governance and the process of rural, social and economic transformations. The students are able to figure out the subtle role of the caste in local politics and local administration. The students have learnt the process of marginalization and exclusion which take place at the village level. Further, they are able to see the interaction between political democracy and social democracy. Village stay helped them to understand the process of democratization. The whole exercise was done through learning process. VVP is a programme which enables the students to exercise group learning and self-learning. The students have gained rich experience in writing reports based on their field-work. The learnt learning methods are many which need proper conceptualization. They used different new methods also which require conceptualization. Their level of sensitivity has been increased when they see the rural reality while interacting with the poor and the marginalized. Apart from the above academic learning they got a sense of responsibility in solving the problems of the society as a responsible citizen. The whole programme enhances the role of citizen's social responsibility.

Notes and References

1. G. Palanithurai, 2012, *Social Relevance of Higher Learning Institutions in India,* New Delhi: Concept Publishing Company Pvt. Ltd.
2. G. Palanithurai, 2009, "Rural Universities in the Era of Globalization", *University News,* Vol. 47, No. 33, August.
3. *Relevance of Rural Institute* a document submitted to the Ministry of Human Resource Development by Gandhigram Rural Institute.
4. G. Palanithurai, 2009, "Larger Role of Academics in Rural Human Life", *University News,* Vol. 47, No. 16, April.
5. Apart from the VPP there are many other activities designed and carried out by the Departments under the rubric of Extension or outreach. G. Palanithurai, 2005, Extension in Higher Education: The Missing Dimension, *University News,* Vol. 43, No. 17, June.
6. Minutes of the 40th Academic Council Meeting held on 25th June, 2012. Gandhigram Rural Institute—Deemed University.
7. The Students can work on the following issues:

Gram Sabha functioning	***Bio-diversity***
SHG Functioning	Anaithu Grama Anna Marumalarchi Thittam
Traditional Panchayat	Thai Scheme
Youth Clubs	Resource in the Panchayat Area
Temple Committees	Social justice issues
Money lending	Gender issues
Livelihood	Differentially abled
Resource available	School functioning
Skills available	PDS functioning

(Contd.)

Politics and social structure	Library functioning
Panchayat function	Writing stories – Transformation
MGNREGA – Stories	Common Property Resource Management
Women leaders in Panchayat	Gap between People and Governments
Dalit leaders in Panchayat	Untouchability issues
People's Audit on (1) Water supply (2) Street light (3) School functioning (4) PDS (5) Health Centre (6) Veterinary Center	

8. G. Palanithurai, 2009, *Empowering People through Empowering Panchayats: Experience in Ten Years in Panchayats*, Gandhigram: Rajiv Gandhi Chair for Panchayati Raj Studies.
   Website: www.rajivgandhichair.org
9. Group I, 2012, *Impact of MGNREGA – A Case Study Analysis*, Gandhigram: Department of Political Science and Development Administration.
10. Group II, 2012, *Participation of People in Panchayat*, Gandhigram: Department of Political Science and Development Administration.
11. Group III, 2012, *Women's Empowerment through SHGs*, Gandhigram: Department of Political Science and Development Administration.
12. Group IV, 2012, *People's Participation in Gram Sabha*, Gandhigram: Department of Political Science and Development Administration.
13. Group V, 2012, *Accountability in Gram Panchayat*, Gandhigram: Department of Political Science and Development Administration.
14. Group VI, 2012, *Transparency in Functioning of Panchayat*, Gandhigram: Department of Political Science and Development Administration.
15. Group VII, 2012, *Service Delivery through Report Card*, Gandhigram: Department of Political Science and Development Administration.
16. Group VIII, 2012, *Traditional Panchayats*, Gandhigram: Department of Political Science and Development Administration.
17. *Times of India*, 16th August, 2012.
18. It is the statement given by the Coordinator of the Programme Dr. Sonkhogin Haokip.

PICTURE GALLERY

Plate 1: Interaction with the Beneficiaries under MGNREGA

Plate 2: MGNREGA—Work Site

Plate 3: Man and Women at work under MGNREGA

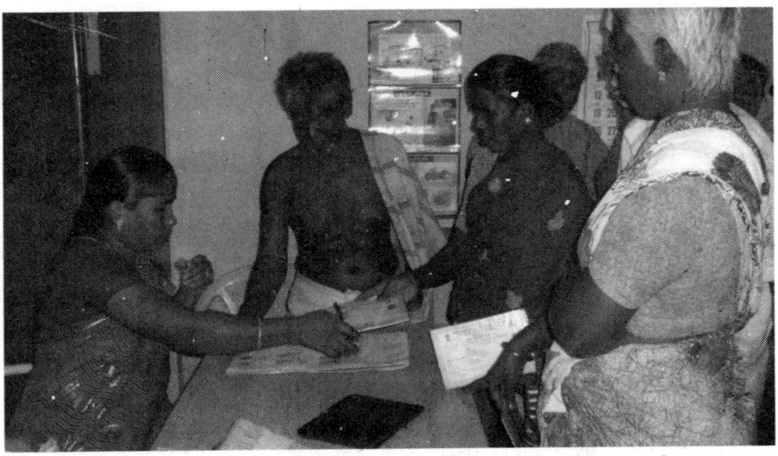

Plate 4: Distribution of wages by the Panchayat President

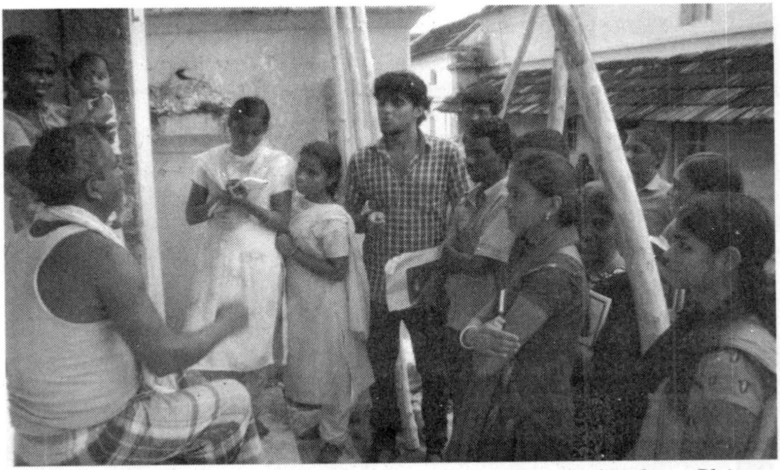

Plate 5: Interaction with traditional Panchayat leader, Chinna Nattaman

Plate 6: Gram Sabha Meeting

Plate 7: Traditional Panchayat leader Nattaman, along with Panchayat President in Gram Sabha

Plate 8: Even though *Panchayat* President is present, her husband sitting among the crowd runs the proceedings

Plate 9: Traditional Panchayat leader Nattaman, giving suggestions for the development of the village

Plate 10: Poorly developed SC area (IX Ward)

Plate 11: Shramdan in the Camp

Plate 12: Independence Day Celebration in the Camp: Students singing National Anthem on occasion of Independence Day

Plate 13: Dr. Sonkhogin Haokip (Camp In-Charge) hoisting National Flag on Independence Day

Plate 14: Independence Day Celebration in the Camp

Plate 15: Students taking Oath on Prevention of AIDS/HIV

Plate 16: Students attending Gram Sabha Meeting

Plate 17: Dr. G. Palanithurai with the Campers

8
New Task for the New Vice-Chancellors

Introduction

Once in India and particularly in Tamil-Nadu Vice-Chancellors were visionaries, and academic giants. Leaders of higher learning institutions were men of upright character, honest, dedicated, and committed and builders of modern India. They were above politics, and they belonged to a cadre of men and women known for sacrifice and dedication. Governments conducted search for such persons and persuaded them to take up such assignments. When eminent persons were appointed as Vice-Chancellors, the above positions have been made as respectable positions. They never preferred to meet governance leaders and in fact governance leaders used to meet them. In such a way, Vice-Chancellor positions had been kept in high esteem and honour. They were looked at with respect and they were free from political interference. They were above the State bureaucracy. They also conducted themselves in a highly dignified way. But now these positions have been transformed as office of profit and as a result, higher learning institutions are in bad shape. Anti-corruption Wing of the Government conducted raids in many of the universities and located needed evidence to file cases against the Vice-Chancellors as they involved in corrupt practices. This kind of news items in the newspapers have given an image to the public that higher learning institutions are deeply afflicted with mal and corrupt administration. To change the existing condition and image, we need a different set of academic leaders. We need a cadre of honest, committed, scholarly and visionary leaders to our higher learning institutions to transform the existing institutions as Institutions of Excellence to compete with National and International Institutions. Higher Education System in India is undergoing a change in terms of its output in quantity and quality due to globalization. Its implications have to be seen in perspective. It has got both positive and negative aspects.

Background

Higher Education System in India has two faces. One is excellence and the other one is poor. One set of public premier institutions are maintaining their standards and the other set of public institutions like universities barring a few have reached the lowest ebb in terms of their standards. In the same way private institutions also have two sets. One is excellent group of institutions operating in a business mode with quality. The other set of institutions have poor infrastructure and poor quality of teachers and as a result they exploit the students. The public premier institutions and some of the private institutions have produced talented manpower needed to the market. Hope rising was done only by these institutions. But in practice, the aspiring individuals who are being drawn towards higher education portal are exploited by the poor quality institutions both private and public. The premier institutions contributing to knowledge economy have made the people to develop aspiration to make quick and instant money. There has been heavy rush for medical and technical education. Students have been made crazy after medicine and engineering as they found money spinning opportunities in those courses. As a result mushroom growth of engineering and medical colleges. Most of the Engineering and Medical colleges are owned by the Politicians. It is a new business venture found out by our politicians. A few of them are with neo-merchant class. Ultimately, the objective of the creation of new institutions is to make profit. Many of them have been created by flouting the established norms, rules and regulations. It is a pity that a student who has secured a just pass with a minimum of passing marks is admitted in Medical colleges and Engineering colleges. Students who are not eligible to get admission in some of the courses in arts and science departments in highly rated Arts and Science colleges are eligible to get admission in Medical and Engineering Colleges managed by the private trusts. In such a way basic minimum qualification for admission to medical and technical education has been lowered. Despite the lowering of basic minimum qualification, seats are available and unfilled in thousands. But in reality the produced manpower from the poorly maintained public and private institutions could not be absorbed in the market as the quality of the manpower produced from the institutions is poor.

While looking at the scenario, one will find sudden expansion of the higher learning institutions and on the other sudden increase of unemployment. But the government has fixed the target for enrollment increase. As a result higher learning institutions have increased more social problems. This is the general trend all-over the country. To participate in knowledge economy and to maintain economic growth skilled manpower is needed to the tune of 500 million in 2020. But the existing institutions are producing graduates, certificate holders, diploma holders, but not individuals with quality skill required to the market. There is yet another issue namely the students coming to basic science and social science disciplines are the rejected lot from the premier institutions and those who are unable to pay the fees in technical institutions. Absolutely for social science, students who have secured lowest marks are coming and joining. It is almost a scholarship academic programme. Here, also only the premier academic institutions get students of high quality. As a result in the process of sudden expansion of higher education with an objective of exploiting the opportunity of entering into knowledge economy and to increase the enrollment rate have caused great damage to the whole system. In the process of expansion of higher education, exploitation has been increased alarmingly. Private players have been allowed discretely without proper screening to enter into higher education as service providers. The service provided by them is substandard and in turn they instead of helping the society, they create problems to the society by producing unemployable graduates. In the given context, making the institutions to deliver the quality goods as per the expectations of the market and society is really a difficult job. Yet it has to be performed.

Leadership Crisis

Many factors are responsible for the poor performance of the higher learning institutions and of which one is obiviously the leadership. Leadership plays a critical and crucial role in shaping institutions and their delivery of services. In Tamil Nadu it was obvious from the observation and statements made by some of the key intellectuals who involved themselves in cleansing the higher education system that Vice-Chancellors had been appointed on political, caste and of late monetary considerations. Once a leading educationist made an observation that highest bidder can get Vice-Chancellor position in the universities of Tamil Nadu. The Vice-Chancellors are also involved in all kinds of corrupt practices which are even not known to the politicians. Because of the corrupt practices, the position of the Vice-Chancellors has been made very weak. Dignity of the post has been lowered. Academics who assumed leadership in the recent past have turned the higher learning institutions as business centres. At present every stakeholder made prosperity by degrading the higher learning institutions. The above statements have been observed by several educationalists and academic administrators. All the above observations have been captured in the newspapers also. Teachers with high integrity and probity in the higher learning institutions could not do anything on this issue as they are individuals and not organized and moreover they did not want to get trouble from the power centre. Other teachers started discussing the issues in public places and end it there itself. Beyond that no one wanted to take up the issue as they are not affected and instead they are also free without having any accountability. Vice-Chancellors in recent times never ensure accountability in the higher learning institutions as they are weak in morality and honesty. As a result, the higher learning institutions are in lower order in terms of production of quality manpower. Pay and Perks of the teachers are very high in the university system. Teachers have never imagined that they would get such huge sum as salary. Yet the Vice-Chancellors could not get best out of them for the benefit of the students as they do not know the way how to extract work from them. The universities are in the lowest ebb in terms of their functioning and delivery of services. But the context requires high capability on the part of the teachers and the efficiency on the part of the functionaries of the higher learning institutions to compete with the global players in terms of manpower production.

Searching for New Leadership

The Twelfth FY Plan approach paper unequivocally argues for quality, inclusion, expansion and competitiveness on the part of higher learning institutions. For sudden expansion the Government of India opens the system for private players to participate and reduce the burden of the Government. While allowing the private players everyone kept the American experience. The models evolved by the Central Government opens the door for private players. All higher learning institutions are put in a competitive mode. The available staff and more particularly the quality staff are inadequate for the expected expansion. So, the continuous upgradation of the quality of the teachers is the need of the hour. The existing higher learning institutions are not in good shape and functioning mode. Against this background one has to look at the process of recruitment of the Vice-Chancellor. So, the universities need visionary leaders with commitment and zeal to transform the universities from deep slumber and inefficiency to dynamic and efficient in their functioning. To perform the above task, a highly reputed scholars with integrity and a sense of commitment have to be appointed as Vice-Chancellors. The new Vice-Chancellors should have vision, commitment, honesty, sense of dedication and courage with a new management perspective and strategy. Tenure given to Vice-Chancellors is only three years. It is a very short period to bring drastic transformation in the university set-up.

New Roles

Absolutely, the new incumbents in the universities have to put the higher learning institutions in a mission and campaign mode to perform the difficult job of making the teachers to work and to enhance their capability to the expected standard. The newly appointed Vice-Chancellors have to give a clear-cut message to the teaching and non-teaching community that the administration and governance under his/her leadership should be open, transparent and work towards efficiency. Quickly road map has to be drawn for contextualizing the academic programmes, research activities and outreach or extension programmes. With the active participation of the faculty members, an action plan has to be prepared. It should be contextual. Equally an administrative reform document has to be prepared with the active participation of the non-teaching staff of the university. Immediately, the teacher's capacity development to the context has to be done with the involvement of the teachers of the premier institutions. For quality research and outreach programmes, systems and mechanisms have to be created and if available they are to be fine tuned. Enormous resources are available in higher learning institutions and they can be extended to the community directly by the institutions themselves. Suitable mechanism has to be evolved and by which outreach programmes and activities can be carried out. In the same way, social relevant issues can be taken up for research. Ultimately well researched issues and the conclusions drawn from the research can be used more effectively for policy advocacy and contributing to Industry. In such a way, research has to be promoted.

While the whole functioning of the institution is transformed to work towards outcome and not output the teachers should not be in panicky. So far the academic system's evaluation is based on the output and now it has to move towards outcome. When the system is moving towards outcome evaluation, teachers have to transform themselves attitudinally, behaviourally and performance-wise. This transformative process should be made easy and for which the leadership has to adopt consciousness management approach. Teachers should feel that they gain advantage in every action in the transformative process. In such a way, message and perception has to be given to the faculty members. Otherwise, the non-performers in the university system are always in group with political lenience and they will make the administration in a crisis mode. If the university goes in a crisis mode creative development works will suffer. In the process of transformation, the performers have to be facilitated continuously and they are to be protected from the disturbances of the non-performers and the performers will be put in group work for the efficient delivery. Public opinion has to be created to the effect that the higher learning institutions are marching towards the new heights in a new direction. Quickly university has to be taken from the bureaucratic web and for which reform initiatives have to be taken to reform governance and administration of universities. The governance and administrative system with higher learning institutions have to be simplified and made transparent. By doing so message has to be given to the stake-holders that the new Vice-Chancellors should have open agenda for total transformation. The available faculty and the facilities have to be used very effectively in all the three dimensions namely teaching, research and extension or outreach.

New Linkages

Our universities which intended to achieve higher goals and outcomes have to be linked with other national and international premier institutions. There are enormous resources both material and human resources available in many premier institutions which are underutilized at present. They are to be used profitably for the advantage of the many stake-holders. In our university system grouping the scholars for a common research task is very difficult for the academic leaders and there is no such vibrant culture developed in our university system even though we had stipulation from the University Grants Commission. Likewise we do not have a healthy culture in the university system to collaborate with other institutions either on project or activity basis. Because the question of who is working under whom prevents the academics to have institutional collaboration. This kind of culture has to be changed by introducing a healthy relationship between and among institutions with a norm of 'working with' and not 'working under'. Functional relationship has to be developed with developed institutions in the west and the north through signing of Memorandum of Understanding (MoU). Signing of MoU should not be done in a ritualistic way. Western universities sign MoU with Indian universities with a clear-cut focus of mutual co-operation. Every university should have an office for international co-operation headed by a Senior Professor. The main duty of the Centre is to facilitate the faculty member to have international collaboration with the faculty members of other foreign universities. The office has to work for helping the students to avail the foreign fellowship. In the university system, it is one of the most important activities of the Centre for international co-operation.

Contextual Programmes

Next to internationalization, appropriate academic programmes contextually designed have to be introduced and existing programmes have to be contextualized and fine tuned. While conducting the programmes extreme professionalism has to be followed. Higher learning institutions have to be made more rigorous and outcome oriented. For this purpose, professionalization of academic programmes is an imperative need. In our country we have professional and non-professional programmes and courses. But to make the students employable, the programmes whether the students are in professional or non-professional programmes, they should be offered in a professional way. Even a non-professional programme could be made a professional one by doing it in a professional way. Sometimes, even the professional courses are done in a non-professional way and as a result the students from the professional programmes could not get employment opportunity even though vacancies are abundant in the same specialisation. That is why we face high rates of unemployability. As long as the higher learning institutions are producing unemployable graduates, the institutions are doing havoc to the society. It is almost a disservice to the society done by the higher learning institutions. Higher learning institutions should not fix only the target, gross enrollment rate, but they should concentrate on high quality production of man power from the institutions. All public funded institutions are conducting conventional academic programmes whereas the private and self-financing institutions are conducting academic programmes based on the requirements of the market. The new Vice-Chancellors have to face volley of problems to change the mindset of the academics to reorient the academic programmes to the requirement of the market and the society.

There is yet another challenge in the higher learning institutions in the present context. Academic programmes have to be fine tuned by incorporating skill oriented courses at least one fourth of the entire programme. Even to offer these skill effective linkages have to be established with industrial houses and other stake-holders who provide job opportunities to the students. The Vice-Chancellors work goes beyond the boundary of the university campuses. The Board of Management has to change the style of functioning. So far the Board of Management are substantially involved in resolving the problem of the staff and internal politics. Now, it has to move away from the mundane works to development and transformative works. Further, the existing teaching mode has to be changed to learning mode and classrooms should be the space to be created by both teacher and the taught. Newer teaching and learning methods have to evolved and used in the higher learning institutions and for which university and college teachers have to be prepared.

All the departments should have high standard academic programmes, research both foundational and action oriented and outreach programmes and for which new research and project culture have to be developed. Teachers have to be sensitized and oriented to take up projects and for which facilitative mechanism has to be developed. Unless the higher learning institutions move away from bureaucratic web, it is very difficult to make the teachers to take up projects. Now, the entire university system is under the control of the clerks and Section Officers. A new outreach unit has to be developed with the available faculty members to carry out outreach programmes. The whole administrative mechanism has to be geared up to support the academic, research and outreach programmes. In this process transparency and accountability in administration has to be maintained.

Reforming Governance

Contextualizing the University Administration is a stupendous task before the university leadership. The bureaucratic system which we have at present in the universities is more obstructionist rather than facilitative. Despite all technological developments, the non-teaching staff of the university system has not come up to the level of expectation. Unless the university non-teaching staff is reoriented and fine tuned to the expected role in the context, it is very difficult to transform the teaching staff to work for new contextual roles and objectives. It is the responsibility of the leadership to enable the faculty members and the non-teaching staff to move faster and work harder to put up the face of the university so strong and vibrant. To perform the above task, a new leader is needed. He or She should be transformative, scholarly, known for administrative ability, open to learn, and eager to advice. S/he should be transparent, responsive, responsible, accountable, and administrative and governance leader. S/he should have needed capacity to exhibit quick change in the style of functioning of the university system. His or her sincerity, honesty, skill and dynamism will be the core for the transformative process of higher learning institutions. To take the university in a new direction, cleaning operation has to be undertaken. Equally teachers and non-teaching staff have to be prepared to perform the task professionally in a changing mindset.

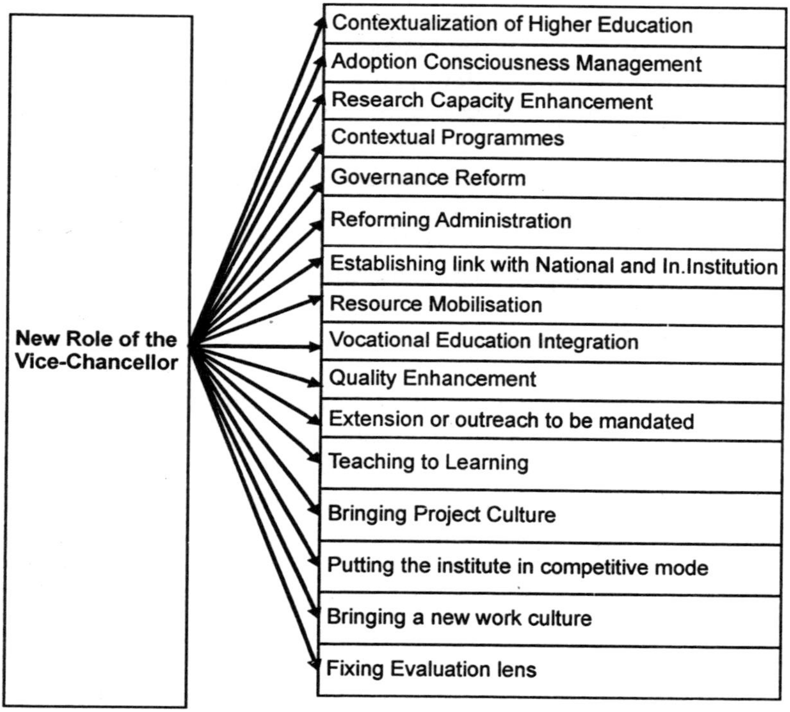

Fig. 8.1 : New role of Vice-Chancellor.

Conclusion

At present we need an extraordinarily a committed, visionary, highly acclaimed scholarly person with contextual managerial ability to take forward the higher learning institutions and to make them to compete with highly rated higher learning institutions in India and abroad. To achieve the above objective, the whole machinery of administrative system and the teaching faculty have to be contextualized and transformed. A contextual vision document has to be prepared with the active participation of teaching and non-teaching staff of the university within a short span of time after assuming office by the new Vice-Chancellor. All the above has to be done quickly. To perform the above task a vibrant leadership is needed. To find such persons to our higher learning institutions as Vice-Chancellors, the search committees have to be really search committees searching for such qualified individuals. Members of Search Committees should be above Board. The existing practice of scrutinizing application has to be given up. The empanelled candidates have to be interviewed by the Chancellor personally and they have to be asked to make a presentation about what they will perform in the university if she/he is appointed. At present, the higher learning institutions are being highly politicized and highly inactive and the new leaders need a strong back-up for their transformative action at the institutions from the State government. By giving a clear-cut message by the State government leadership, the newly appointed persons will be able to move forward to take steps to transform the higher learning institutions.

9
Where We Lead in Higher Education

Introduction

India is known for several paradoxes of which one is the way her higher education institutions are responding to the challenges of the twenty-first century created by the globalization of the economy and making use of the opportunities to achieve prosperity and contribute to a knowledge economy.[1] To make use of the new opportunities, the higher education institutions have to adapt fast to the emerging trends.[2] In the process of making use of the opportunities, threats have affected and afflicted the higher education system, ultimately creating a crisis in India. Originally, the higher education system was created with the objective of creating knowledge and disseminating the same for the purpose of helping society to move to higher level activities.[3] But now the higher education system has been reduced to producing students as marketable products instead of creating ethical, informed and enlightened citizens. Students now enter the higher education institutions by paying huge amounts as fees and emerge with the mindset that they have to get back the money which they have invested in this education. As a result, the economic principle of demand and supply works in the higher education system too. Ultimately, the issues which have affected all other sectors have affected the education sector also.

To address the issues and the problems in higher education, steps have been taken by the Central Government by appointing committees and by organizing conferences, workshops and consultations. The committees and conferences have prepared reports[4] which have ultimately created a confusion as to which direction and with what approach and perspective we are going to move in higher education in India. From the reports one can easily identify the contradiction between the Government and the University Grants Commission. No doubt the reports have brought out the issues afflicting the system and suggested remedial measures. But the reports have also produced contradictions between schools of thought in the Government itself and among the scholars involved in preparing the reports and among the institutions involved in policy-making.[5] The present write up tries to underline the current crisis in higher education and suggest ways and means to evolve a framework to regulate higher education in India.

Context

Globalization has created unprecedented opportunity in the economy and the same can be exploited only by creating needed manpower. The condition of the higher education system in India is one of need for more partners to invest in higher education so that the needed manpower can be created for the market. The Governments cannot find adequate resources for investment in immediate expansion in higher education. As a result, it has no other option but to allow private players in the higher education system. India has got a tradition of private players in the higher education system. But, now, it has become a business venture. Previously, from the days of the British, private players came forward as their social responsibility to support the Government and the society to increase the enrollment of students in higher education. But now the context prompts the private players to take up roles in higher education not as corporate social responsibility, but purely as a business venture to make profit and more profit by making use of the new opportunities to prepare manpower for global demands.[6] Even if it is a business, it can provide quality manpower suitable to the market. But it is not done and this ultimately creates the current problem.

Since, education is in the concurrent list, both the Central and the State governments could have developed a framework through which the new institutions could have been regulated systematically to function as partners of Government to produce manpower. Unfortunately, the old system of screening continues to function and thereby the new institutions were screened and they were allowed to play their role. All the institutions were thoroughly examined as per the existing norms and, on the basis of the recommendations, deemed universities status was given. Justification was given by the Chairman of UGC.[7] This opening of creating deemed universities was thought of because of the existing rigid system of higher education. Hence, everyone moved through the deemed university route. Originally, deemed university status was conferred for uniqueness or for specialization. It is normal that any sudden expansion needs a new institutional mechanism and, in the absence of the new, the old one has to be equipped to meet the requirements. In India, there was no new institutional set-up nor any expansion of the existing mechanism to cope with the increased opportunity. As a result, corruption crept into the system. The whole higher education system is choked by corruption and has not delivered the goods needed to the economy, and as a result, people are exploited and it has added to the unemployment problem rather than solving the problem.[8] For all the ills afflicting the higher education system, the poor performance of the regulatory mechanism which supervised the functioning of the higher education institutions is responsible.[9] Liberalization has been used to liberate the whole process of supervision by dubious means and thereby private business groups have entered into the education market. As a result now we find in the education market one set of high class institutions with all facilities and qualified staff performing the task of producing the manpower needed for the economy. This set of institutions has helped the cream of the society. Entry is highly restricted to the elites. Yet another set of institutions has been created with inadequate facilities and poor quality of the staff. They also lure the aspirants and send them as products to the market. But they cannot be absorbed in the market. As a result we find a crisis of unemployment. Here it is to be noted that one cannot ignore the role played by the private players in higher education in enrollment of students.[10] Of the institutions, both Government aided and managed and private managed, which segment creates problems and what are the problems they create, are to be analyzed in an integrated way. In all sectors we find problems while opening the avenues for private. We have taken decisions to tackle all those problems. In the same way, we try to find out suitable ways and means to correct them. But a word of caution that education sector connoted be treated like telecom or power or transport sector. To understand the whole problem, primarily we have to analyze the issue contextually, institutionally, managerially and functionally.

Classification of Institutions

In India we have a multiplicity of institutions. The first set of institutions are funded by the Government and they are adequately equipped and cater to the needs of the competently equipped students. They are IITs, IIMs IISs and nationally recognized institutions. They produce quality products on a limited scale but not to the requirements of the market in terms of quantity. These institutions have not grown physically to produce the needed quantity of manpower for the market. There is another set of public institutions which cater to all segments of the society. The facilities are moderate and the staff are qualified but not up to date. These institutions have performed moderately in producing quality products. This set of institutions are facing paucity of funds. Contextual change has not been effected in their programmes. They are the State universities and Government colleges. Absolutely accountability is weak and it is a free ride for politicians through Government. The third set of institutions were started long back with the assistance of Government grants, but under private management. The programmes are updated periodically and accountability is maintained despite inadequate facilities. Some of the institutions have changed their programmes periodically as they have got autonomy from the university system. They are Government aided private colleges.

A further set of institutions is totally new. They are of two types. One is those started with commercial interest on a permanent basis. These institutions are well equipped and well established. The above institutions are professionally maintained to meet the market requirements. They are in the market. They are professionally equipped and well maintained and scientifically administered. Another set is purely temporary and driven by profit motive with poor quality of professionals, inadequate facilities with poor staff strength. This set of institutions will function as long as they fetch profit. The moment the market crashes they will quit higher education and move to new businesses just as they came to this sector. Now, we hear the news about the sale of colleges and institutions. It is because of the commercial nature of the institutions. Having judged the surging aspirations of the middle-class and the poor for higher education and the existing weak and corrupt regulatory mechanism these new institutions have entered into the market. Table 9.1 shows the details of the institutions in the higher education domain.

Table 9.1: Institutions in the Higher Education Domain.

Sl. No.	*Type of Universities*		*Number as of 31-5-2009*
1.	Central Universities		40
2.	State Universities		235
3.	Deemed Universities		
	Government	41	
	&		
	Private	86	
	Total	127	127
4.	National Importance (State)		05
5.	National Importance (Centre)		33
6.	Private Universities		39
	Total		**479**

Source: University Grants Commission.

Responding to Market Needs

In the context of expanding opportunity, the first two sets of institutions have not expanded to the level of requirement with increased public funding because the Government has to invest heavily in primary and secondary education. The third set of institutions have maintained the *status quo,* but there is no initiative for expansion of quantity and enhancement of quality. The institutions which have been maintained by private charitable organizations have expanded the scope of intake but not improved the quality.

The first set of institutions have improved themselves and contextualized yet they cannot meet the market requirement of manpower. The second and the third set of institutions have not improved and contextualized their functioning and their programmes of activities. These institutions are functioning under the framework of the bureaucratic system and they enjoy very limited autonomy. Even within the autonomy given to the institutions needed changes could have been effected, but unfortunately it was not done as the institutions had poor and weak leadership and there was no social commitment on the part of the academics. The academics do not have professional pride, with a few rare exceptions. Hence, they could not respond to the challenges of the new dispensation of globalization.

The fourth set of institutions have responded to the challenges by creating institutions with needed facilities, and professionals. They have performed the production of students in terms of quantity and quality. There is yet another group of institutions in the same fourth set quickly entered into the market with pure business motive produced students in quantity without quality expected from the market. In this category, a large number of institutions were started with a profit motive even by selling old business units. All the established norms have been dismantled by these institutions. Both the types of this set of institutions have tried to escape from the ambit of the Government regulations by making use of a provision to confer deemed university status and thereby these institutions are made autonomous. They want to escape from the control of the State Government to increase the intake of students and to collect fees from the students without any question. The conditions are favourable for this move because the first three sets of institutions have been facing a multiplicity of problems which detracted those institutions from repositioning themselves to cope with the new demand from the market for manpower. Academic and research programmes have been introduced as they find market and fees have been fixed arbitrarily and the whole process is a free ride. Many of the institutions do not have required facilities and qualified staff and yet they fix fees at higher levels. Absolutely, there is no regulatory mechanism. It is true that even regular State and Central universities are also not having a regulatory mechanism. At least in the Central and State universities' executive bodies, Government representatives are made members. Moreover, the Central and State universities have fixed fees and intake of students. They cannot violate those norms. They may not be able to produce quality manpower to the required quantity. The problems of the State universities are managerial, administrative, governance, financial and so on. Hence, the fourth set of institutions have utilized the weak points of the first three sets, of institutions and entered into the domain as free riders. They have created problems by exploiting the people by setting up the sub-standard institutions and extracting huge amounts of money from the students and producing students of poor quality far below the expected standard of the market.

Remedies

In order to streamline the problem afflicting the higher education institutions, the Government of India has constituted committees and produced vision documents. They are Knowledge Commission report, University Grants Commission report and Yashpal Committee Report. All the reports were prepared during the UPA regime. The report of the UGC was prepared through a lengthy process of consultations and stakeholders' participation. The other two reports are good reports, but elitist in orientation and approach. It is to be noted here that education is not a central subject or a state subject, but is in the concurrent list. But a substantial number of State Governments have not taken serious steps like the Federal government to revamp the system. Instead the State Governments have used this opportunity to add confusion and alleged that the Central Government has taken away the power of the states on the subject of education since, it is in the concurrent list. All the three reports, though they contradict one another, underline the need for revamping the whole higher education system. The discussions were on governance, management, financing and innovation. The focus is on expansion, inclusion and excellence. This focus is due to the expanding market for more human resource, to include the underprivileged and hitherto excluded into the system and to achieve excellence in higher education. It is a process of competing with other countries in supplying quality manpower to the economy and to make profit through a knowledge economy. Based on the observations, and recommendations steps have been taken to correct the maladies in the system.

Manpower Need

The whole target for expansion is not based on the realistic assessment of the manpower requirement of the world and the country in particular. The very function of higher education institutions is to produce skilled and capable manpower for productive activities in the economy and to create new knowledge. For a balanced economy, manpower planning is an imperative. The higher education system will play an important role in improving the economy and reducing the social problems if the supply and demand match. Manpower planning and human resource preparation have to be managed thus. But in India both are not done very scientifically. The moment the private players sensed the gap, they filled in the gap by organizing institutions and the whole process was quick and hence all kinds of problems arose in the higher education system. The poor quality of higher education is due to unregulated institutions and poor quality of human resource production which ultimately exploited the people and caused unemployment problem in the society. A social menace has been created by these institutions. Against this background, the remedial steps are on. For this remedial action strong political will is needed as the majority of violators and profit seekers in the higher education system are politicians of the lower order and businessmen of the lower order. Ethical politics and business will not create any such problem as we face today in India. Private players are in higher education system in the West also. They are not facing such problems as we face here. These groups have not only created problems through their institutions, but also corrupted the entire political and bureaucratic class and thereby the other three sets of institutions have also been disturbed managerially, administratively and in other modes.

Analysis of the Issues

To overcome the above crisis one has to look at the problems broadly and systematically. The problems cannot be simplified and narrowed down to mere commercialization or privatization of higher education. Further, it is to be seen contextually, historically, institutionally and functionally. By doing so, one can locate the problem in the structural, policy, administrative, financial and functional domains. The whole issue started when the higher education domain expanded due to the requirement of manpower due to the increased demand in the market both in India and abroad. So, expanding the higher education institutions was an imperative need. Expansion requires huge investment in the higher education sector for which the Government did not have adequate resources. Even in the normal course public institutions will not mend or amend according to the contextual change quickly on their own however autonomous they are. The stakeholders in the public institutions tend to think that system maintenance and *status quo* maintenance will be the safer course of action. It is only the market force which will act fast to respond to the challenges and changes of the context. Hence, the Government allowed the private players to come in.

In the existing arrangement of institutions, namely the first two sets of institutions, there was no possibility to meet the new demand. Hence, necessarily private players had to be allowed. In this process, two groups of private players entered. One group deliberately planned to stay on in this sector and made their institutions professionally competitive. It appears that their strategy is to put the service in business mode. There is yet another group, purely a commercial venture to exploit the demand at the quickest possible and as long as possible and there is no long-term interest. They are racketeers. They do not have any ethics and their entry into the higher education system has destabilized the whole educational management system in India. These groups make profit on the aspirations of the emerging new middle class and the ignorance of the poor. The second type deliberately mobilized huge resources and sometimes closed their earlier ventures by selling their industries and invested in higher education institutions. In the sudden expansion all have moved into the domain by utilizing the weak regulatory mechanism which was already corrupted.

Despite proliferation of institutions and production of students on a massive scale, the market requirements are not met qualitatively. The market requires skilled manpower. But institutions could not produce not even one third of manpower acceptable to the market. As a result, a large chunk returned to the unemployed army and remained unemployable. The reason for the inability of the new institutions to produce quality manpower is basically due to the poor quality of the teachers. The newly created institutions could not find quality staff from the market for the sudden expansion. To attract the students, the institutions have used the names of luminaries in the field fictitiously. The products of all the institutions were absorbed in the market as the market was expanding. But the slowdown in the economy naturally ejected a chunk from employment. The ejected were from the bottom of their recruitment. Despite the slowdown of the economy and the ejection of employees from the market, the institutions have not regulated their functioning. They continue to produce their products as unemployables. So, a mismatch has emerged between the market demand and the supply of personnel from the higher education institutions.

In the first and second set of higher education institutions, much change was not effected and hence, they remained as they were. They could not increase their intake. Hence, for the aspirants and for the market, there was no choice excepting relying on the private players. It is to be noted here that it is only the private institutions that have substantially enrolled students in higher education institutions and substantially produced graduates for the market needs. It is because of the foul players that the higher education system has got mixed up and got into trouble. Simply because of the troubles we face one cannot wish away the role of the private players in the higher education system.[11] So, these issues cannot be dealt with as in the telecom sector or other sectors. How to classify the private as good and bad? It can be done only through a rating of the private institutions. Further, a minimum standard has to be set through a regulatory mechanism. We have regulatory authorities, but in the sudden expansion the regulatory authorities could not expand their activities. The evils of globalization have affected this sector as they affected the other sectors. As a result, the regulatory authorities remained nominal heads rather than becoming effective instruments regulating the higher education institutions. The regulatory authorities have been corrupted. These are natural when sudden expansion takes place in any sector. The whole world is deliberating on new regulatory mechanism for economy after seeing the fall of the market economy.[12] We witness the same in higher education. How to regulate the institutions to perform their task perfectly, professionally and profitably for the advantage of the individuals concerned and the country is now the question.

The new target fixed for enrollment in higher education system in India by comparing other Asian countries and

Western countries requires new institutions. When the Governments are not able to find resource for expansion, it is a welcome move to involve private players. When private players are coming into this sector in the context of the market economy one cannot expect the same values with which private players started institutions through their charities at the dawn of Independence in India. The old private players had come to serve the society by sacrifice but the new players have come to the higher education sector not with the objective of serving the society *per se*, but the new *mantra* 'Serve and Prosper' quite against the old *mantra* 'Serve and Sacrifice'. Even with this new *mantra* "serve and prosper", there is nothing wrong in it if the products coming out of the higher education institutions are getting opportunity in the job market by equipping themselves. So, the new *mantra* is applicable to all.

But the question is whether the newly created private higher education institutions have performed their role professionally to meet the market demand. When we look at the newly created institutions in terms of their performance, the performance of the other set of the institutions starting from the second set has to be evaluated systematically. Because even traditional universities funded by the Government, colleges run by private charitable institutions and by the Government are deeply affected by a series of problems and as a result they are also producing unemployable substandard graduates. Some of the newly created deemed universities are far better than some of the public funded full-fledged State universities and deemed universities. Hence, the mess is in the whole system, not only in the newly created deemed universities. To set right the maladies, a comprehensive framework enforced through a well regulated mechanism is needed. Occasional outbursts and arbitrary evaluations and hasty decisions will not solve the problems. Instead they will create more problems. So, a series of steps are needed now to revamp the higher education institutions. Primarily, the Government institutions and Government aided institutions have to be well equipped in terms of facilities and faculty. One cannot presume that the public funded universities and colleges are all having qualified staff. Of course, they are qualified educationally, but they are not professionally equipped.

The political interference in the universities and the colleges have effectively prevented the entry of qualified and professionally competitive staff and as a result substandard personnel have entered into the higher education portals as teachers through dubious means. Hence, a thorough evaluation is needed for public funded institutions also. The intake capacity has to be doubled after equipping the institutions infrastructurally. Along with this, the shift system has to be introduced and then the market demands can be met. Secondly, the private institutions which have got adequate facilities have to be made full-fledged universities. Some of the deemed universities are far better than some of the State universities. Hence, their elevation to the level of universities is an imperative. Thirdly, the private institutions which are lagging behind have to be regulated and they should be allowed to take in only a minimum number of students till they equip themselves infrastructurally and human resource-wise. To overcome all these problems, two regulatory authorities have to be created. One is for conduct of examinations and the other one is for collection of fees. For the above two tasks two institutional set-ups have to be created. All institutions, private, public, quasi public, aided etc. can run programmes for which they will be autonomous, but examinations have to be conducted by an independent agency.

By doing so in the competitive process, the weak institutions will fade away from the market as the market mechanism will work. Secondly, the fees for programmes have to be collected only by an independent agency which has to collect the fees and remit the same to the institutions based on the number of students admitted. By effecting this regulation, the present exploitation of the people can be avoided and standards can be maintained through the common examination system. Instead of creating chaos and confusion with a careful selection from a battery of solutions the higher education system can be revamped and saved from deep malaise and the same can be made powerful engine to produce professionals for the market rather than producing students to join the unemployed army.

Conclusion

The existing problems in the higher education system are many of which exploiting of the people by the institutions and production of poor quality of manpower are the most important and serious. Setting up of an appropriate higher educations system, evolving of a new higher education policy, creation of an appropriate regulating mechanism and allocation of adequate resources are very essential at present. Further, it is not merely the evaluation of the deemed universities alone that is needed. A comprehensive analysis of all sets of institutions is an imperative. The existing regulatory mechanism has to be made more rigorous and transparent. While evaluating the performance of the institutions, the outcome should be the indicator and not the output. While evolving an evaluative framework, multiple frameworks have to be evolved to suit the requirements of the institutions based on different sets of objectives. Further, an independent agency for fees collection and examination system will eliminate many of the evils which have crept into the higher education system.

Notes and References

1. J. Salmi, 2000, *Tertiary Education in the 21st Century: Challenges and Opportunities,* Washington DC: World Bank.
2. Anthony Stella and A. Gnanam, 2004, *Looking Ahead: A Decade of Accreditation in Retrospect: Development in Quality Assurance of Higher Education in India,* Bangalore: Aicra Publishers.
3. International Commission on Peace and Food, *Developing Human Resourcefulness,* California: International Commission on Peace and Food, 1989.
4. *National Knowledge Commission: Report to the Nation 2006;* UGC, *A Brief Report of the National Conference on Development of Higher Education,* October, 10-11, 2007; and *Report of the Commission to Advise on Renovation and Rejuvenation of Higher Education,* 2009.
5. Thomas Joseph, 2007, "Commission *Versus* Commission in Higher Education" *Economic and Political Weekly,* December 15, p. 20.

6. R. Ramachandran, 2009, "University Business", *Frontline*, July, 17, p. 4.
7. T.K. Rajalakshmi, 2009, "The Increase Explained: Interview with S.K. Thorat, UGC Chairperson", *Frontline*, July, 17, pp. 14-15.
8. Ravi Sharma, 2009, "Main Markets", *Frontline*, July, 17, p. 25; S. Viswanathan, "Tamil Nadu", *Frontline*, July, 17, p. 27.
9. R. Ramachandran, 2009, "It has to be a Constitutional Body: Interview with Yash Pal", *Frontline*, July, 17, pp. 22-23.
10. M. Anandakrishnan, 2007, "Critique of Knowledge Commission", *Economic and Political Weekly*, February, 17, p. 558.
11. Pawan Agarwal, 2007, "From Kothari Commission to Pitroda Commission", *Economic and Political Weekly*, February, 17, p. 555.
12. Edward J. Balleisen and David A. Moss (Eds.), 2010, *Government and Markets: Towards a New Theory of Regulation*, Cambridge: Cambridge University Press.

10

New Paradigm of Social Science Research in the Era of Globalization

Introduction

Role of academics in higher learning institutions becomes a subject of debate among the intelligentia after the controversial convocation address of Narayanamoorthy in the Indian Institute of Science, Bangalore recently. He raised a fundamental question whether our scientists have made any worthy contribution to get the recognition of the world. It triggered arguments, not only among the scientists but also among opinion-makers and policy-makers. When it is debated a few argue that he chose to make this statement to provoke our scientists to plunge into action. Yet another argument is that he refused to look at the contributions made by our scientists and without looking into it he made a sweeping statement which is condemnable. There is yet another argument that he raised this question only to make our scientists to introspect consciously whether they have discharged their roles and responsibilities. It is always my habit to generate views, opinions and ideas on all issues of society from ordinary villagers as a teacher committed to society through our academic activities. I took this argument to a villager. He asked me to raise a question whether the scientists have any concern for the poor who are in the villages. Our scientists have gone to moon but they have not visited a village to educate our people to lead the life by following science and technology. Had they come to villages, sanitary conditions would have been improved a lot and thereby poor would have learnt the art and science of leading a decent human life. It is unfortunate that scientists who hailed from the rural areas have migrated to cities for career and they never turned towards villages. The above observation made to write this chapter.

In this context, articles have been written about the achievements of our scientists to prove that Narayanamoorthy is at wrong.[1] While doing so, the authors have indicated the publications and other contributions of our scientists. At the same time they have indicated the failures of the Government in providing sufficient funds for research in India. There is yet another related question to be answered is to what extent our scientists have done justice to the investment made however small the investment is in research and development.[2] While these argument are on the social scientists have been kept out as if they are not connected to this discourse. The question raised by Narayanamoorthy is more relevant to social scientists than scientists as they have been mandated to connect themselves with the communities and society by using scientific and technological innovations. In my opinion his question is applicable to all those who are in higher learning and research institutions. Since, I belong to social science discipline, I would like to introspect from our own discipline perspective.

Backdrop

Against this background, one has to ponder over the status of social science research and the institutions as they have to play a key role in policy shifts at present as society witnesses unprecedented changes due to globalization, democratization and decentralization. Social science disciplines in the higher learning institutions and research institutions barring a few are not in a sound footing qualitatively and quantitatively. The conditions and capacities of these institutions are not to the level of the requirements and expectations despite their expansion.[3] In the neoliberal political regimes our country is able to enhance its economic growth to the unexpected level of 9 per cent but it fails to perform in distributing the benefits of growth to the people more specifically to the poor despite its earnest efforts by bringing rights revolution.[4] For the past three decades we have been witnessing a series of measures to enable the market forces to work more effectively and vigorously to achieve higher growth by utilising the new opportunity of economic globalization and at the same time there have been checks created to market forces. In the meanwhile, to protect the poor, there have been series of safety nets introduced by the Central Government. While seeing the above activities in the backdrop of the neoliberal framework, one would find the contradictory positions of the Central Government. Free market exercise under neoliberalization negates social expenditure and establishing social nets. Many appreciated the pro-market initiatives of the Federal government and at the same time, they have criticised the government for its stand on the pro-poor. There are a few appreciated the Federal government for its pro-poor stand. But they are not loudly communicated as they are not able to fix the State under specific category of welfare state in the new context. The implications of the safety nets established through acts and schemes with huge outlays have not been evaluated integrally all-over the country. Researchers could have concentrated much on the issues of exclusion, marginalization, inequalities, deprivation and inequities in the context of massive outlays on safety nets for the poor.

Context New

In the above given backdrop, one could notice the abolition of the Planning Commission with an aim of strengthening the planning process at the local and regional levels and creating of (Niti Aayog) for evolving suitable policies instead of detailed programmes and schemes with huge resource allocation for poverty reduction. It is being widely perceived as an anti-poor measure of the Central Government by various adversaries. Because so far all pro-poor programmes and schemes have been chalked out only by the Central Government and heavy outlay has been given to all these measures only by the Central Planning Commission. The Central Planning Commission was perceived as an institution meant for poor as it has carried out extensive research on poverty reduction and evolved many schemes on poverty reduction. Hence, its abolition has been made as a contentious issue being debated in all fora. The Central Government has taken a position that the Centre need not do all these activities as communities are far away from the Central Government and the Central Government cannot evolve solutions to micro-problems, issues, and problems which vary from region to region. Hence, solutions needed at community level and regional level need not be addressed by the Central Government. Experience shows that despite the earnest efforts of the Central-Lanning Commission micro-problems had not been solved as expected. Because India is not a small country and it is almost a sub-continent and variations are huge. India has got different faces. One could see the face of a poor African country and a rich Western country in India.

By proliferating schemes for poverty reduction with elaborate details regarding the operational strategies, the Planning Commission took over the responsibilities of poverty reduction which is not worthy attempt on the part of the Central Government by keeping huge resources at the level of Central Planning Commission. Corrupt practices have been developed in the process of delivering the schemes to the stakeholders. People who involved themselves as brokers to take development schemes and programmes from Government departments to the people who have to get development benefits.[5] They are the middlemen between the Government and the people. Development brokers have emerged in the context of widely prevalent information gap. This development brokerage has to be eliminated through development activities at the grassroots level by active involvement of the people as stakeholders. Large number of middlemen are involved in the corrupt practices in the development sector as people are not having enough information and knowledge about the process of development. Under neoliberal framework state should become minimal and market has to be given a free hand. It is also seen that the market led activities have not reduced vulnerability and it tend to exclude more number of groups from the mainstream development. In the process of accelerating the speed of the economic growth depletion of natural resources are faster. As a result, poor become the victims of the faster growth. In the same way, the tribals are driven out from their place of dwelling as vast natural resources meant for growth activities are only in the forest where tribals are living. The gap between the rich and the poor has been increased. Global wealth data book confirms the gap between rich and the poor.[6] In the same way, gender gap sounds the alarm bell. Yet another problem is the exclusion of the poor and the *dalits* in the process of fast expansion of higher education in India.[7] That is why a new concept "inclusive development" becomes prominent in the academic discourses. This concept "inclusive development" is frequently used in World Bank literature which is being subsequently used by the Governments. Inclusive activities have to be done only at the community level. But it becomes a problematic one. Even the SC and ST sub-plan has not been done in many of the states in India.

Larger Implications of Central Finance Commission

In the new context under neoliberal framework, the Central Government increases revenue share from 32 per cent to 42 per cent to the State Governments. In the same way, the 14th Central Finance Commission has increased the allocation quantum jump to local bodies for development planning at grassroots. Huge money is going to flow from the Central Government to local government with minimum conditions. This Finance Commission has made a recommendation that the entire money has to be devolved to *Gram Panchayat* alone. On an average a *Gram Panchayat* will get at least Rs. 85 lakh for a period of five years. When it is compared with previous Finance Commissions, this time *Panchayats* are getting three times more than what they got during the previous period. Yet another striking point is that the amount is going to be transferred only to *Gram Panchayat*. The amount has to be spent for basic amenities.[8] Adequate amenities have to be created for *Dalits* and women from this amount. Evolving micro-plan for development at village *panchayat* level and conducting social audit are the two mandatory activities have to be carried out to get the funds in successive years. The money has to be spent on social development activities both in hardware and software. When elite capture is the reality in many of the states, what will happen to the huge money is a known fact. It is an established fact that corruption has been reduced and people involved in corruption have been increased after the establishment of the Panchayati Raj institutions in India.[9] In this context, one can imagine what will happen to this money?

Marked Departure

On the one hand, the Central Government has come to a conclusion that it has to work for economic growth by accelerating the pro-market activities. On the other hand, it feels that countervailing force could be created at the bottom right from State Government to local Government for establishing safety net for the poor. The argument for the shift of responsibility from the Central Government to State and local government is that thirty years of neoliberal policies have increased the inequality among the regions, states, districts, castes, religion and ethnicity despite high growth and adequate allocation of resources for social development activities.[10] It is to be noted that despite the enactment of laws to safeguard the rights of the poor, conditions of the deprived and marginalized have not improved as expected. Hence, it has come to a conclusion that planning for well-being of the people could be done only at the State and local Government levels.

The Federal government while looking after economic growth through market economy and looking after the poor through social policies and development schemes has increased enormously its workload, but it did not increase its capacity to manage. As a result, one could see in poor outcome of the development initiatives through huge schemes and programmes and mismanagement of the delivery units and it led to increased rent seeking culture in the economic and political administrative system. Hence, it is being advocated that the Federal government should be slim and its governance has to be enhanced. "Less government more governance" came because of the new context. In the past three decades aspirations of the people to acquire material benefits increased enormously as market economy induced the culture of consumerism. It has not only weakened the Government and its performance, but also it weakened the democracy as workload of the Central Government has increased enormously. Managing the Government machinery becomes problematic. Here, one has to realise the fact that in India, the social conditions are always not conducive for promotion of democracy. In India we are in institutional democracy, but not in behavioural democracy. Agrarian economy, caste hierarchy, patriarchy, feudal practices are always acting as barriers to the growth of democracy.[11] Poor quality of democracy will reduce the quality of governance and administration.[12] Democracy and development have to take place at the grassroots by the active participation of people.

Democracy Promotion

Democracy is a higher form of political activity which requires informed citizens with responsibilities. Even today we are in minimal democracy with inbuilt weaknesses. All our political activities are confined to institutions. Behaviourally, most of the Indians are feudal. Unless the behaviour of the people is changed, our democracy continues to be in institutions and ultimately we will miss the core values of democracy. Thus, democracy has to be deepened and for which promotional activities have to be undertaken. Along with globalization and decentralization, democratization has become a wave in the past three decades in the world. All the three are movements in the world. Promotion of democracy is also a major activity of the democratic countries in the world. In India, we have seen only political democracy. To achieve social democracy we have to struggle a lot. The plea of Dr. B.R. Ambedkar in this regard is still in our agenda. University teachers, students and researchers have to join together to create awareness about the true values of democracy. Apart from awareness creation, universities can conduct workshop for the local body leaders to build their capacity to involve themselves in promotional activities. Social science departments can serve the MLAs and MPs through backend office to enrich the service of the people's representatives. Researchers and teachers can assist the representatives of the people in conducting micro-research in their consistencies.

Planning from below for Development

Democracy promotional activities and participatory development have to be done at the community level. Both activities can be carried out through a planning process. But the task is not so easy. In the past two decades though it was mandated barring a few states most of the states have not prepared the local bodies to develop prospective plan for development. To address the above problem, the new Government at the centre plans to leave the planning to the State and local bodies. At present the State planning machinery though it exists, its condition and capability is not commensurate with the expected tasks in the new context. An issue related to bringing households under BPL list is going to be left to the decision of the State Governments. It requires more research space and decision-making powers at the State planning commission level. It should have the capacity to give direction to the State Government departments to chalk out schemes and programmes for social development. Equally, it should have the capacity to help the local bodies to evolve development plans from the community level with the active participation of the people. At present, the planning machinery at the grassroots is only a nomenclature. Beyond that it has not been developed into a full-fledged planning unit with needed infrastructure and scientific manpower.

For any decision-making data base is very essential. In India always data generation takes place only at the district level. Data collection, validation and updation have to take place from *Gram Panchayats* to State governments level. Scientific way of collection and validation of data are very rare at micro-level. Classic example is that the State Finance Commission reports say that paucity of scientific database made the commission to make appropriate recommendations not accurate recommendations. This will prove that we are weak in data management. Unless they are being looked into scientifically and made effective, the money flow to State Government and local governments will be wasted enormously.

It is always a practice in India that the Central Government is blaming the State Governments for their poor management of resources and in the same way local governments are being blamed by the State Governments for their poor management. National governments are being blamed by the World Bank and hence, it promoted the concept 'good governance' and by which good governance is interpreted as effective resource management by using power. In order to overcome this shortcoming, a considered suggestion was broached. It is nothing, but planning from below to work on demand of the people. Hence, attention has to be given for the involvement of the local populace in the process of preparing a plan document at the *Gram Panchayat* level. To reform the planning process at the State level and local level, series of steps have to be taken. On the one hand, huge responsibilities have been bestowed on the State governments by saying that Centre cannot work on all development issues and it will facilitate market to achieve high growth. It argues that it will devolve more resources to the State, but work for the poor and marginalized is the responsibility of the State Governments. Further, it says that it gives broader policy guidelines and it is the responsibility of taking the development schemes to the poor to suit the requirements of the local conditions. The local bodies are the operational level in the field that they do not have the needed professionalism to carry out the workload.

Micro-Action Research

At present, to achieve inclusive development, we need only action at the micro-level. For micro-level activities we need more professionals. We need research at micro-level and for which we need newer methodological nuances to be adapted to conduct micro-studies. As a follow-up of micro-studies micro-planning exercise has to be done. Where is institutional mechanism for micro-planning? In the given context, Government machinery cannot be expanded and it has reached its maximum. In the neoliberal framework Government has to be reduced governance has to be increased. Hence, all the above activities have to be carried out only by some institutional mechanisms available nearer to the community. All the above have to be done by the support of the higher learning institutions. It is the only available option at present as the available civil society organiszations do not have the capacity and wherewithal to do that exercise.

To work with community at the grassroots, all grassroots institutions need manpower for action research and to carry out field activities. Preparing professionals to extend hand hold support to community and to carry out action research are the main tasks of higher learning institutions. New development practices are to be introduced at the community level. Activities from poverty reduction to tackling deprivation and marginalization have to be carried out at the level of community. It has to work for resilience building. These are all specialised activities to be done at *Gram Panchayat* level. These specialised activities can be carried out by only professionals. Expertise can be drawn only from the higher learning academic and research institutions. Academic institutions linking themselves with such development activities in the society through governance institutions will enhance the capacity, skill and capability of the students and teachers.[13] But the existing conditions indicate that the higher learning institutions have not oriented and prepared themselves for the new tasks. Hence, the social science faculties have to reorient themselves to work for the community.[14] Their repositioning and reorientation will alone make them eligible to perform the above tasks.

Community Mobilization

Our society has to be prepared to lead a decent dignified human life by following science and technology. Majority of the people in India mostly in rural areas lead life in subhuman living conditions. Even to maintain basics like maintaining sanitation and water supply communities find difficulty as they have no knowledge, awareness and sensitivity on the issues which affect their life. There is a vast gap between scientific practices and societal life. Classic example is that an individual is having a mobile phone spending five hundred rupees per month but the same individual indulges in open defecation. Poor sanitation is due to poor adoption of science and technology in life. Our community is far away from scientific practices. A community or society which is not adopting science and technology in their life cannot lead a scientific decent human life. Who will bring the community to science or science to community other than educational institutions? It is only the educational institutions which have to educate not only the students but also the entire community. Students are the best instruments to communicate to the communities by changing their attitude and behaviour. But in India one cannot see much impact in the society in terms of the behaviour and performance due to the presence of educated persons in the community. Externally, man and community have been changed and internally they remain where they were. Community has to be prepared, oriented and sensitised through massive mobilization[15] by the higher learning institutions.

Data Generation and Management

For any decision-making whether it is at macro-level or micro-level data base is imperative and important. Many of the failures of development initiate is attributed due to poor data base. For scientific management of development data base is very essential. But at present in India data collection becomes a problematic one. The classic example is the recently conducted caste census survey done by the Ministry of Rural Development, Government of India. It is being questioned by many as it has got several weaknesses.[16] Till date there is no data generation mechanism at the bottom or ground at the community level. We have census data, NSSO data, and they are all generated for decision-making. When governments emphasise planning at the grassroots, data collection becomes very vital. Every *Panchayat*, every block, every municipality, every corporation should have strong data base. Data collection tools can be developed, improved by research institutions, but the data collection works can be done by the higher learning institutions functioning very near to the *Panchayats*, blocks, municipalities and corporations. Data enumeration work has to be done professionally. It could be done only by the higher learning institutions.

At the *Panchayat* level or at the municipality level or at the corporation level household data can be collected and they are to be constantly updated for continuous decision-making. They are to be analysed continuously. By analysing the data families which are at deprivation and vulnerable can be identified. Each and every Panchayat or municipality or corporation should maintain data about the vulnerable families. Socio-economic data of the local units can be analysed.

Yet another issue namely the implications of climate change need local action. Disaster preparedness, disaster management and disaster mitigation have to be done only at local level. The local bodies, have a role in all the above activities. They are to be performed by the local bodies but the local bodies do not have the wherewithals. Hence, they require supportive organization. Now, more number of activities have to be done at community level. The local bodies need the support of knowledge institutions. From data collection to evolving local department plan, local bodies need the support of the higher learning institutions. Now, the higher learning institutions have to concentrate on the issues of local areas and they have to conduct research on all those issues. Here, it is to be remembered that it requires funding for higher learning institutions. Already they are chasing for money to run the institutions.[17] Apart from the above, they have to help the local body institutions to prepare development plan. The above activities can be coordinated through systematic outreach activities in the rural areas.

Since massive fund transfer is going to happen to local bodies through State Governments for development activities, one would envisage more professional scientific work at the grassroots which require huge manpower for generating data for micro-planning. In India, we have around 500 departments in 400 public funded institutions specialises in social science branch knowledge and 2,52,000 teachers are working in the same discipline. Apart from the above, we have 200 social science research institutes functioning with the financial support of the Government. In our country grassroots civil society organizations are as effective as the civil society organizations work at national level for policy advocacy. The

Box 10.1: Who will take care of the young widows?

Madapalli a small village in Vellore district has got 200 widows and of them majority are young poor widows. They have to look after their siblings through their earnings. Of them more than 90 per cent are the victims of alcoholism. It is wide prevalent in the village as the village is traditionally involved in brewing and selling country liquor. After the Government of Tamil Nadu lifted the ban on liquor sale, they switched over to company liquor consumption. The president of the village *Panchayat* Mr. S. Rajendran admitted the fact that these women are worst affected due to consumption of alcohol by their husbands. Now a solution has to be found out to rehabilitate the families. It could be done easily by forming self-help groups (SHGs) among the widows and provide opportunity to them to build their skill. Once it is over, they should be enabled to make entrepreneurial ventures by providing bank loan which could be possible only through evolving a micro-plan for the development of the families and groups in the village *Panchayat*. It could be done by an educational institution preferably higher learning institutions locked very near to the *Panchayat*. In a village *Panchayat*, a micro-level plan could be developed and for which anyone of the social science departments could be involved. While preparing a plan for whole village, a sub plan could be prepared for these widows affected due to alcoholism. The National Rural Livelihood Mission scheme could be used for this purpose. "Liquor Robs Life, Bread as Vellore Village crowded with 200 Widows", **The New Indian Express**, 8th August, 2015.

work that exists at the *Panchayat* levels are of many types and the needed support for *Panchayat* is for a longer time. It is almost handhold support as all the works are technical in nature. By working with the communities the social scientists and students of higher learning institutions would gain substantially. Apart from the above policy community will gain substantially in this process.[18]

Box 10.2: Who will prepare administrative manual for panchayat administration?

Both Governments (Centre and States) have manual for administration. Whereas the local governments have no such manual. After seeing the plight of the *Panchayat* leaders, the Department of Political Science, Gandhigram Rural Institute prepared a manual for *Panchayat* administration for Tamil Nadu. The manual was published by the Concept Publishing Company Pvt. Ltd., New Delhi in English and same in Tamil was published by South Vision in Chennai. The Tamil edition of the manual has undergone five revisions. After seeing the manual Government of India has asked us to prepare a model manual. By joining with Kerala Institute of Local Administration, we have prepared a model manual and submitted to the Government of India. In the same way, the Department of Public Administration in anyone of the universities in the respective states can prepare an administrative manual for the respective state local bodies as there is no such manual in many of the States in India. It is very essential for efficient administration. Even the manual can be uploaded in a website and matters can be downloaded by anybody for his or her use.

Conclusion

Need of the hour is repositioning our research and higher learning institutions to establish organic linkages with State Government and local governments for conducting extensive research at micro-level to reduce poverty, deprivation and marginalization of groups from mainstream development. All macro-problems pertinent to socio-economic development could be tackled effectively and efficiently at micro-level by using the local governance machinery with the active participation of the stakeholders. All the activities have to be done scientifically by applying efficient management models. These activities have to be done by the local bodies, but they will do only if they are being assisted by knowledge institutions. Likewise, democracy promotion activity has to be done at the community level. Beyond electoral politics and electoral mobilization, people have not been conscientised on the values of democracy. This conscientization process has to be done only by such higher learning institutions. Further, they have to extend handhold support to prepare micro-plan and for which data gathering and analysis have to be done by these institutions on a sustainable basis. State governments can allocate some portion of resources for such action research continuously by the research institutions and help the local bodies to take decisions and prepare plans. This kind of linkages will help the Government departments to carry out their activities professionally and the universities, colleges and research institutions to strengthen their research capacity and bridge the gap between the book view and field view. This kind of organic linkages will strengthen the academic programmes because of the extension component integrated in the syllabus. All the higher learning institutions both universities and research institutions have to act as resource agencies for the local bodies.

Notes and References

1. Pallava Bagla, 2015, "From Basket Case to a Global Force", *The Hindu* (Sunday Magazine), 2nd August.
2. Vijay Chandru, 2015, "Revamping India's Scientific Eco-System", *The Hindu*, 3rd August, 2015; Pulapre Balakrishnan, "Swaraj and Substance in the Academy", *The Hindu*, 4th August.
3. DFID, Social Science Research in India: A Mapping Report, New Delhi: South Asia Research Hub, 2011; ICSSR, Restructuring the Indian Council of Social Science Research (Report of the Fourth Review Committee), New Delhi: ICSSR, 2007; M.S.S. Pandian, "Social Science in South India", *Economic and Political Weekly*, Vol. XXXVII: No.5, 31st August, 2002.
4. S.K. Das, 2013, *India's Rights Revolution: Has it worked for the Poor?* New Delhi: Oxford University Press.
5. G. Palanithurai, 2007, *Vision of Rajiv Gandhi on Local Governance*, New Delhi: Concept Publishing Company Pvt. Ltd.
6. Mihir Shah, 2015, "Tribal Alienation in an Unequal India", *The Hindu*, 4th July.

7. Sukhadeo Thorat, 2015, "A Blue Print for Higher Education", *The Hindu*, 11th August.
8. Government of India, 2014, Fourteenth Finance Commission Report, New Delhi: Government of India.
9. James Manor, 2010, "Local Governance" in Niraja Gopal Jayal and Pratap Bhanu Metha (eds.), *The Oxford Companion Politics in India*, New Delhi: Oxford University Press, p. 66.
10. Sanchita Bakshi, *et al.*, 2015, "Regional Disparities in India: A moving frontier", *Economic and Political Weekly*, 3rd January.
11. Rajini Kothari, 2005, *Rethinking Democracy*, Hyderabad: Orient Longman, pp. 90-123.
12. Philip Keefer, 2009, "The Poor Performance of Poor Democracies" in *The Oxford Handbook of Comparative Politics* (eds.), Carles Boix and Susan C. Stokes, New Delhi: Oxford University Press, pp. 806-909.
13. G. Palanithurai, 2015, *Students in the Field: An Experimental Learning Village Placement Programme*, New Delhi: Concept Publishing Company Pvt. Ltd., pp. 65-74.
14. T.S. Papola, 2010, *Social Science Research in Globalising India: Historical Development and Recent Trends*, New Delhi: ISID Working Paper.
15. Madhu Purnima Kishwar, 2005, *Deepening of Democracy: Challenges of Governance and Globalization in India*, New Delhi: Oxford University Press.
16. M. Vijayanunni, 2015, "Where is the caste data?" *The Hindu*, 15th July.
17. Dr. Ramamirtham Gopal, 2015, "The Great Funds Chase", *The Hindu*, Education Plus, 3rd August.
18. Mathur, 2009, *Policy Research Organizations in South Asia*, New Delhi: IDRC.

11

Quality Enhancement in the Higher Learning Institutions

Introduction

No one will dispute over the argument that there is a correlation between quality of education and economic development and equally quality of education and quality of life. Now, quality becomes a *mantra* in everybody's lips as people and policy-makers keep an eye on the expanding job market for professionals in the world due to globalization of economy and increasing aged population in the West. Under new public management regime efficiency and effectiveness are the two important determining factors in influencing the human activities to reach the targeted goals in the context of change.[1] Every nation is interested in achieving demographic dividend and for which the countries are in the preparation of youth as workforce in the world of works.[2] The workforce needed to the world of work is professionals.[3] Equally countries which are involved in assisting other countries wherever youth are available for the preparation to the world of work, by building the skill and capacity, to fulfil their workforce requirements have started their work in skill building exercise for the youth.[4] But ultimately harnessing the benefits depends on the quality of manpower production. Whether it is skill or knowledge, quality is the need of the hour. The whole exercise depends on the quality of higher learning institutions. Quality of the institutions could be seen in their structure, culture and craft. In the context of change, all the three aspects have to be reframed and repositioned to meet the requirements. The changes that take place in the market compel every other segments reform themselves to harness the benefits. Of them education is one of the key sectors enabling the process of development. Hence, education institutions have to reframe the structure, evolve a new culture with a set of new norms and develop skills suitable for professional works.

An array of steps are needed to create quality higher learning institutions. They are infrastructure, staff, process and leadership. Of the above factors process is more important and vital as it enhances the quality of skill, capacity and capability of the individuals who are coming out from higher learning institutions. It is to be understood properly that the educational institutions are involved in the activities of transformation of the students both internally and externally. Educational institutions are transformative institutions. The students have to be transformed attitudinally, behaviourally and performance wise. The transformation has to take place both internally and externally. It is a difficult and tough task. Essentially, it envisages the utilization of the infrastructure facilities by the students and teachers, engaging the students by the teachers and teachers by the students and evaluating output of the institutions.[5] It is a continuous engagement process to be done organically and consciously. Since India keeps a complex system of higher education, finding a quick solution to the existing problems and more particularly the production of unemployable graduates from the higher learning institutions and poor quality of research is not that easy. It is a country with extreme regional variations, social and economic inequalities and cultural differences with multiple governance mechanism and public policies with powers to deal with subjects have posited volley of problems to the policy-makers to evolve a suitable policy for imparting quality education. To keep India together, integrated and democratic all kinds of deviations have to be tolerated and allowed. Now, time has come to respond to market by producing employable students. An issue arising out of the above presented conditions is finding solution through one fit framework and it is extremely difficult. Yet one has to try for that if there is any option.

Context

Having seen the prosperity achieved by some individuals by making use of the new opportunity created through globalization both in India and abroad by acquiring higher degrees in higher learning institutions, everyone is tempted to invest hard earned or borrowed money in higher education irrespective of their economic status to get gainful employment either in India or abroad. Contextually, the Government is also interested in harnessing the benefits and hence it is trying to fix target for enrollment of students in higher education to participate in knowledge economy despite its poor investment in higher education.[6] Having seen the potentials in higher education people who are closer to power have started investing in establishing private higher learning institutions mostly technical and professional with an aim of making profit as they get in business. People who created educational institutions from preprimary to private university at present belong to third generation. The third generation is known for profit seeking. One could see competition among educational entrepreneurs in using this opportunity to maximize the profit.[7] Higher education becomes a very big business. From a small town to cosmopolitan city people started investing in establishing educational institutions not with the aim of helping either the Government or society, but to get maximum profits as they get from other business ventures. All kinds of violations of regulations and rules by both private and public aided institutions are visible. The classic case is (Vyapam scam) in Madhya Pradesh. It is not only in Madhya Pradesh, the same kind of practice could be noticed in many of the States in India which is going to be unearthed through the investigations of CBI. As a result, instead of preparing the students to the world of works, a large number of educational institutions in both categories (Private and Public) are involved in issuing certificate religiously. In India, issuing certificates becomes a ritual or a ceremony. Really certification is a process. It is not an ordinary process. It is a rigorous process. It is a transformatory process. In reality one could not see such rigour in the educational process in India. Impact of the expansion of higher education could be seen in increasing enrollment rate, increasing unemployment problem, increasing profit for private educational institutions, lowering the quality of education. Above all it created much complication in the educational sector. Certificates become commodities rather than skill, capacity and capability. Now, it is time to come out from all the problems and more particularly to produce students from the higher learning institutions from saleable perspective in the job market with skill and capacity.[8]

Backdrop

Rising aspirations among the middle class and lower middle class, to make wealth through this new process of the job markets created through globalization, enabled many to take risk by borrowing money and invest in their children's higher education with a hope to get lucrative job after acquiring the degree from the higher learning institutions. India has witnessed sudden expansion of higher education to meet the new requirements in the market. For the sudden expansion, policy climate was favourable, infrastructure expansion was fast, but the institutions found shortage of quality manpower. In order to meet the conditionality of the regulatory bodies in the absence of quality staff all corrupt practices have been developed. It is found out in the investigation large number of names of the teachers found in more than one institution. It is a truism that whenever any sudden expansion takes place the first causality will be the quality. Within a few years of the expansion exercise of higher education one finds huge unemployment army coming out from technical institutions after acquiring technical education. It is unequivocally argued that all the students who are coming out from the higher learning institutions with certificates are not qualified skill and knowledge-wise and majority of them are unemployable as per the observation and assessment of the employees who are in industrial and service sectors.

A newspaper advertisement is a testimony to the existing reality. Two advertisements came in a Tamil Daily in the same page for the recruitment of brota master (a cook preparing *roti*) for a hotel on the National Highway with a salary of Rs. 500 with perks per day. Next to the above advertisement there is an advertisement to recruit a junior engineer was given by a small company by indicating Rs. 12000 as salary per month. It is a pity that the salary of a *roti* maker is more than the salary of a junior engineer. Aspiration to acquire material wealth has been increased in geometric proportion and it is the outcome of globalization. But to fulfil the aspiration everyone believes that it could be done only through skill and capacity. Increasing skill, capacity and capability will enable the individuals to enhance their earning. It could be achieved only through education. But the educational process today in the higher learning institutions has not transformed the individuals as expected and for which many reasons are attributed and of which examination and evaluation is crucial and critical. Passed out students from the higher learning institutions are coming out in large numbers to the world of work, but they are stagnant without getting any employment opportunities. This scenario has baffled the parents as they have invested huge money in their sons and daughters with the hope that their children will be placed comfortably in industrial and service sectors. Even after seeing this pathetic conditions, colleges are giving advertisement in the newspapers that hundred per cent placement is assured. For educational institutions students are the brand ambassadors. But now the educational institutions follow the model of industry in giving advertisement. All educational institutions have created a market division. A paid person is working full time to look after the marketing activities of the institutions.

Yet the newly passed out students from plus two in schools are not in a position to believe the assurance given by the educational institutions. Because they are seeing the graduates coming out from the technical education are not able to get employment opportunity profitably. The above conditions result in poor turn out to engineering colleges in Tamil Nadu this year. Many engineering colleges are on sale and are to be closed. But general manpower need is not declining. In India, students have been treated as jobseekers and from that only student have been oriented. They are not only jobseekers, but also job makers. It is a well-known fact that such a kind of perception students, parents and institutions have developed. In India an argument is projected that entrepreneurship is the creative work of certain castes in India.[9] This is the condition of higher education in Tamil Nadu. The needed quality manpower could not be produced in our higher learning institutions. It is to be noted here that in the countries of European Union have lifted their ban for recruitment of skilled personnels from Asia. Huge opportunity is available in the West for skilled persons. At this juncture, one has to look at the target fixed by the knowledge commission for the expansion of higher learning institutions. It envisages 1500 universities have to be created by this time. But we have only 712 universities. Before we reach the half of the target we feel the complications have been created in educational sector in the process of expansion. Here, yet another important issue has to be noted. In the process of expansion of higher learning institutions, large numbers of students from the marginalized segments of the society have been excluded.[10]

Establishing a New Mechanism

At this juncture, Government of India is contemplating to bring a new education policy as it finds only an old policy evolved in 1986 and updated in 1992 which could not address the problems what we face in the higher education system at present. While in the process of evolving a comprehensive educational policy quality is being insisted as one of the vital areas to be focused. Job market has unequivocally demonstrated that it provides opportunity for the skilled persons. There is no dearth of employment opportunity. Despite the presence of institutions more in number, quality manpower could not be produced. It becomes a complicated problem in India.[11] It has to be seen from the structural and functional perspectives. In the proposed new education policy quality is much focused subject for debate and discourse. It is being reiterated by the UGC through its documents. Hence, it is being taken up for a brief debate. For this debate, I discussed this issue with students, teachers, marketing managers of private engineering colleges and some of the retired vice-chancellors. In my interaction with them, a number of points emerged and of them one is examination reform. Even while making clearly in their argument that standardization is the only way to help our students to acquire skill and knowledge and thereby they will be enabled to place themselves in the job market at global level.

If quality is to be achieved, without any hesitation and beating around the bush, the Federal government has to introduce one major reform boldly which will change the entire system topsiturvily. It requires a strong will on the part of the Central Government as education being in concurrent list. First the higher learning institutions have to be liberated from the conduct of examination. Today, all the higher learning institutions substantial time and resources are being spent only in conducting examination and issuing certificates. Equally, teachers are spending substantial time in the examination related activities. At the same time one could notice no substantial change and reform done in the examination system. From the first commission, the Radhakrishnan Commission report to till date one issue which is being debated elaborately and which draws the attention of everyone is the examination reform. In the same way, although in the past six decades advocacy has been done for examination reform nothing was taken seriously. Despite repeated emphasis of this reform, this was the most neglected one in the Indian educational system.

Huge time and resources are wasted in the name of examination in higher learning institutions. Teachers' time could be used productively in teaching and research. Teachers have to be relieved from this task in the university system. When examination system is taken out from the university system, an alternative mechanism has to be found out. But it should be for the whole country. To conduct examination for the students of the country in higher learning institutions, whether they are from the Indian Institute of Science, or the Indian Institute of Technology, or the Central universities, or the State universities, or the deemed to be universities, from certificate course to post-doctoral programme, a centralized examination commission has to be established like that of the Election Commission of India. This common system of examination for the whole country will standardize the quality of evaluation. Structuring the system becomes problematic. This could be based on the Indian Election Commission. Indian Election Commission is one of the much appreciated commissions in the world for its efficiency in handling the complex election process in India. The election manual is the key instrument for its success. In the same way, the Indian Examination Commission has to be established. Along with the above an examination manual has to be prepared. The manual should be a speaking manual guiding everyone who are involved in conducting examination and it will explain the procedures and process of conducting examination.

By keeping the examination process away, the role of higher learning institution is to provide only teaching learning opportunity to the students. Testing the student's ability, skill, capacity, capability and knowledge can be done not by the higher learning institutions. Certification will be done by the Indian Examination Commission and not by the educational institutions. From certificate course to post-doctoral degree programme it is only the Indian Examination Commission will conduct the examination and issue certificate. The certificates will bear the stamp of Higher Education System of Indian Republic. It is a highly standardized process as we conduct JRF, NET and Public Service Commission examinations. Despite a few small weaknesses this centralized examination for NET and JRF has brought some quality. No one can dispute over it. All the examinations have to be conducted in the same way. It requires only standardized machinery. The higher learning institutions have to design only the academic programmes, and conduct the same. Beyond it they have to do research. Hence, every higher learning institution has to involve itself in three core activities namely teaching, research and outreach. Once they design academic programme, the programme design should go to the Examination Commission office. The Indian Examination Commission will start designing examination process. The designing of the examination process will be a lengthy, elaborate and tough process. It is the responsibility of the Indian Examination Commission to set question papers, conduct examination, evaluate the answer sheets, declare results and issue certificates. It should be only one agency involved in the job in the whole country. Its wing will be in every state like the chief electoral officers for every State for Election Commission of India.

Higher learning institutions have to issue certificates as the courses have been completed by the students. Beyond that they have no role in evaluating the students and rank them. Further, the Indian Examination Commission has to establish its regional offices. For the whole of India there should be only one system, one procedure, and one scale to evaluate and rank the students. When such an examination system is established, the whole confusion prevails over on the quality of the degrees, mal practices, quality enhancement, and standardization will be sorted out. But the task is not so easy. It is not mere shifting of the controller of examination office from the university premises to a new place. The whole process has to be changed. The above reform shifts the activities from the clerks to the intellectuals. One should not presume that the examination system will be under the control of the clerks as we see today in the university system. As we find academics in the higher learning institutions, we find academics in the examination commission also. In the whole country subject specialists have to be identified and they are to be involved in setting the question papers. The question papers have to be scrutinized by another subject specialist and evaluation has to be done by subject specialists.

Institutional Structure

It requires new institutional structure, functioning process and a thorough change in preparation of manual to conduct examination for the students in the higher learning institutions. If the examination system is separated from the university system, the game is altogether a different one. Both jobs are very tough. Teaching and learning will become a tough process as examination is not in the hands of the teachers who teach the subject in the university. Equally, the conduct of examination is also tough as it would reflect the capacity, capability and skill of the students. For the effective and efficient conduct of examination, the teachers who are in higher learning institutions have to work hard to frame the syllabus for the subjects they teach in a different way to suit the requirements of the Indian Examination Commission. The present system of examination revolves around teachers. It is teacher centric not students centric. The whole system of transaction is teaching centric and not learning centric. In the present system teachers are in safe zone and the whole system is not facing any challenge. Teachers are well protected in the system as lots of safeguards have been created in the higher learning institutions.

The new system proposed will create lot of challenges to the higher learning institutions. The academic work starts at the higher learning institutions while conceptualizing and designing the programme (here programme means from certificate to post-doctoral degree). First detailed programme objectives have to be codified. From there, for each course in the programme, course objectives have to be fixed and from course objectives detailed syllabus have to be prepared (here course refers to papers). While preparing the syllabus teaching methodology has to be specified. In the syllabus itself every detail has to be specified including references for every unit of the syllabus and every module of teaching. There should not be any ambiguity in this regard. Transparency has to be maintained in syllabus preparation. Every aspect should be made explicit. It has to go module by module covering the entire syllabus. The entire syllabus has to be broken into uniform units. Each unit has to be broken into modules of teaching and learning. All these details have to be specified as in election manuals. An even hour of teaching has to be explicitly mentioned in the syllabus so that question paper setter will understand better the load of the unit. In each module, clear references have to spell out. In each module how many lectures are designed has to be indicated to show the depth of teaching. There are certain modules earmarked for self study.

From the above, one can easily gauge where emphasis has been given what is the depth of the subject. Programmes and courses have to be designed only by the subject experts and not by the teachers involved in teaching. Accredited subject experts will be inducted into the programme design boards and they will prepare both programmes and courses. Programme and course design should contain pedagogy also. The teachers those who teach the subjects should understand easily the objectives and methodological nuances to be adopted to teach the courses. There should not be boards of studies for each and every department. When the syllabus goes to the National Examination Commission, it is the responsibility of the commission to set question papers in such a way that whether the students have acquired the skill, capacity and capability as mentioned in the course objectives and programmes objectives have to be evaluated. While setting question papers, question paper setter has to look into the whole process detailed in the syllabus. While setting the question paper, the examiner has to first look into the programme objective and course objectives and then they have to prepare question papers. From the perspectives of the programme and the course questions have to be asked. It is not a small task but a tough and professional task. Questions have to be set in such a way that the answers for the question should reflect the course objectives.

It is to be underlined in the evaluation process that whether the students have acquired the capacity and skill as mentioned in the programme and course objective after undergoing the course and programme should be focused. Question paper setting is a tough task to be done by the experts in the subject and not by the subject teachers who teach the subject. Remuneration for setting question paper has to be given in an attractive way to involve the experts. At present it is not an attractive job and many did not evince any interest on it because of the poor honorarium. Experts are not involved in evaluation process not only because of the poor honorarium but due to the mechanical nature of the work. Hence, the whole process of question paper setting should be made more organic in nature. The whole examination has to be conducted by the officials of the Indian Examination Commission in the respective universities or higher learning institutions. It does not mean that in every college or every university, the examinations will be conducted. Examinations will be conducted in the institutions in which adequate infrastructure facilities are available. The higher learning institutions have to provide infrastructure facilities to the examination commission for the conduct of examinations. Once examinations are over, the process of evaluation has to the conducted.

The whole examinations process is conducted in a standardized format applicable to all-over India. If a student is undergoing certificate or diploma course in tourism, the syllabus for that programme evolved is applicable to all-over India. Whether the programme is offered in New Delhi or in Tamil Nadu, it is one. In the same way, the evaluation process is also the same. For the question paper setting and evaluation, the Indian Examination Commission has to invest huge money as it is to be done professionally. Professionals of high competence have to be involved in this process. Now, the evaluation process in the higher educational system is weak and more specifically it is being attributed for the lack of adequate resources for investment in evaluation. Never experts are involved in evaluations and question paper setting at present. They are mere teachers involved in question paper setting based on text books and syllabus.

Needs Investment

Since, industry and service sectors need quality manpower for their companies, the companies can invest resources on this mission under corporate social responsibility. If standardized evaluation process is in position, high quality products can be easily identified from the higher learning institutions. By doing so, a real competition will be there among the higher learning institutions. Each and every institution will be in a challenging path in preparing the students through a rigorous academic engagement. In this process, many of the fake institutions automatically will disappear. In our country many of the academic programmes are useless, many of the courses are irrelevant and they are being taught as we have teachers on those subjects. Many of the programmes and courses are made irrelevant because of the ways and means they are being taught by the teachers. Through the new examination reform, irrelevant teaching and irrelevant teachers will disappear over a period of time. Teacher's increment, promotion and continuation depend on their performance. Many of the incompetent institutions will disappear automatically. In this process of evaluation, the teachers have to work for their survival and thereby a development struggle will take place. Now institutions are involved in job fetching race for their students to lure the students for their institutions. The role of educational institution is to prepare students for workforce. Getting a job is the responsibility of the students. Now, it is the responsibility of the higher learning institutions to get job offer for their students.

If quality products are coming out from the higher learning institutions, it is advantageous for the industries. There will not be any branding of the institution; it is only a certificate from Indian higher education system. By doing so, mediocrities have no place in higher learning institutions. In order to prepare students for highly competitive examinations, institutions need only quality teacher. These universities and college will look for quality teachers to prepare quality students. Hence, there will not be any bribe in getting appointments in the higher learning institutions and equally the institutions will get high quality leader to guide the institutions properly. By doing this reform at one stroke quality will be ensured, employability will be increased and corruption in higher learning institutions will be eradicated. It requires 'will power' on the part of the Government and it requires huge investment. It is time to radically restructure our higher education and higher learning institutions. Globalization has accelerated the speed of transformation and to cope with the new requirements, the higher learning institutions have to reposition themselves. For this purpose introducing such a kind of reform is a big step in a right direction.

Conclusion

In the new education policy attention has to be given in examination reform. From 1948 to till date uniformly experts asked for examination reform and yet it is not considered seriously. It is not being given serious thought by the policy-makers and governance leaders. Even academics have not given much attention on this issue. As a result, small changes have been introduced in the examination system. They are incremental and *ad hoc,* but they are neither organic nor systematic. Changes are fast in the world at present. To the changing conditions, the institutions have to be repositioned and restructured. In this context, to standardize the certification process and to ensure quality in human power production, a new examination system and process have to be created. Indian Examination Commission has to be created as an independent body. The whole examination system has to be delinked from the higher learning institutions. For the whole country only one Examination Commission has to conduct examination for the academic programmes from diploma to post-doctoral programme. The higher learning institutions need not concentrate on examination work. It will be a great relief for the higher learning institutions and they can concentrate much on research and teaching. Teachers in higher learning institutions have to discharge three responsibilities namely research, teaching and outreach activities in a balanced way to ensure quality in this work.

Notes and References

1. Dolly Arora, 2000, "Public Management Reforms", *Administrative Change*, Vol. XXVII, No. 2, and Vol. XXVIII, No. 1, January-December, pp. 3-19.
2. Dilip H.M. Chenoy, 2014, "Star Scheme to Catalyze the Skill Eco-System", *The Indian Journal of Industrial Relations*, Vol. 49, No. 3, January, pp. 363-366.
3. Liv Mjelde and Richard Daly (eds.), 2009, *Working Knowledge in a Globalized World*, Berlin: Peter Lang.
4. Mathias Pilz and Dipl. Kffr, Sarrah Pierenkemper, 2014, "Apprenticeship Programmes—Lessons from Germany and German Companies in India", *The Indian Journal of Industrial Relations*, Vol. 49, No. 3, January, 2014, pp. 389-400; International Conference on "Youth in Transition: VET in Times of Economic Crisis" organized by the University of Cologne, Germany on 22nd, 23rd and 24th September, 2014; Federal Institute for Vocational Education and Training, Germany is preparing its team to help other countries to enhance vocational education and training.
5. NAAC is doing this exercise to grade the institutions. It does all the jobs only to enhance quality in higher education.
6. Knowledge Commission, 2009, *Report of the Nation 2006*, New Delhi: Knowledge Commission.
7. Arup Majaratna (2014), "Invasion of Educational Universe by Neoliberal Economic Thinking: A Civilization Causality?" *Economic and Political Weekly*, Vol. XLIX, No. 37, 13th September.
8. P. Agarwal (2009), *Indian Higher Education: Envisioning the Future*, New Delhi: Sage Publications, pp. 227-230.
9. P. Kanagasabapathi (2012), *Indian Models of Economy, Business and Management*, New Delhi: PHI Learning Private Limited.
10. Sukhadeo Thorat (2015), "A Blueprint for Higher Education", *The Hindu*, 11th August.
11. A. Viramani (2002), "A New Development Paradigm: Employment, Entitlement and Empowerment", *Economic and Political Weekly*, Vol. 37, No. 22, pp. 2145-2154.

12
Conclusion

From my own experience and experience of others who are working in the higher learning institutions, teachers can do enormous activities in the institutions and outside institutions to safeguard the interest of the public institutions for the sake of serving the poor. For everyone who works in public institutions can discharge both kinds of responsibilities. One set of responsibilities is assigned and those are mandatory in nature. There is yet another which is assumed. Both have to be discharged organically. Once, teachers in higher learning institutions in India fought for their own cause. They have faced harsh conditions in 1960s and 1970s. Through their associations they fought for their rights and entitlements. They had nation-wide agitation and struggle to get their entitlements realized. Now, they are safe. But they have to work for the poor and other marginalized segments. That is possible only through safeguarding the public institutions as public institutions are the only source for the poor to make use of them for their upliftment. Time has come to introspect their activities in the higher learning institutions. Of course, there are problems which are due to political interference, poor funding, poor leadership and poor quality of staff recruited for teaching. Teachers in higher learning institutions have certain social responsibilities. They cannot abdicate their responsibilities. The ills what we found in the public funded institutions have to be corrected and for which like minded teachers have to struggle. Apart from the struggle, the teachers have to perform their duties and responsibilities perfectly and professionally. For a conscious teacher there are assigned responsibilities as they are mandatory. There are certain discretionary responsibilities, which are not mandatory, but they are to be carried out for moral or ethical reasons. Teachers in higher learning institutions have to perform three tasks namely—teaching, research and outreach or extension. Teachers are basically researchers. In social science, they have to perform the task of researcher, they have to take up socially relevant issues for research. In the same way, they have to organize academic programmes based on the need. Socially relevant courses have to be designed and offered. Through the outreach programmes, they have to reach out to the communities. Each and every department or a centre or a school is a specialized one in terms of creating knowledge and dissemination. Hence, their specialized knowledge could be communicated to different type of stakeholders who are in need. Unless the teachers are performing all the three essential assigned tasks, they cannot claim that they are conscious teachers. While performing the tasks they should be organic in nature. All the three functions—teaching, research and outreach—are integrally linked to reinforce each other and hence the teachers have to perform all the three functions.

In social science the teachers in higher learning institutions have to perform the three roles effectively and efficiently and thereby meaningful policy formulation could be done. At present more problem one could see in governance, economy, poverty reduction, administration, social transformation, and mitigating deprivation. All those issues could be tackled only through a meaningful socially relevant research. In the context of globalization, problems have been complicated and complex. Intensity of the problems is also more. To understand the problems new methodological nuances are needed. With the help of new methodological nuances problems arose out of globalization have to be studied. They are to be done professionally. While doing such research streams of researchers have to be oriented and trained. In this process, the teachers, researchers and students have to develop perspectives. Students coming from such marginalized communities have to be shaped, oriented and conscientised on the issues of marginalization. Thus, the teachers in public higher learning institutions should be the trustees of the institutions in performing the duties and responsibilities to safeguard the interest of the institution and by which they can protect the interest of the poor. The need is determination, will, commitment and passion on the part of the teachers.

Bibliography

Altbach, P.G., 2001, "Higher Education and the WTO: Globalization run amok", *International Higher Education,* Vol. 23.

Anandakrishnan, M., 2007, "Critique of Knowledge Commission", *Economic and Political Weekly,* February, 17.

Anandakrishnan, M., *"Privatization of Higher Education: Opportunities and Anomalies",* paper presented at the conference on Privatization and Commercialization.

Arora, Dolly, 2000, "Public Management Reforms", *Administrative Change,* Vol. XXVII, No. 2 and Vol. XXVII, No. 1, January-December.

Balleisen Edward, J. and Moss David, A. (Eds. 2009), *Government and Markets: Towards a New Theory of Regulation,* Cambridge: Cambridge University Press.

Bagla, Pallava 2015, "From Basket Case to a Global Force", *The Hindu* (Sunday Magazine), 2nd August.

Bakshi, Sanchita, *et al.,* 2015, "Regional Disparities in India: A moving frontier", *Economic and Political Weekly,* 3rd January.

Bhargava, Pushpa M., 2015, "For a Renaissance in Indian S&T", *The Hindu,* 28th March.

Balakrishnan, Pulapre, 2015, "Swaraj and Substance in the Academy", *The Hindu,* 4th August.

Chenoy Dilip, H. M., 2014, "Star Scheme to Catalyze the Skill Eco-System", *The Indian Journal of Industrial Relations,* Vol. 49, No. 3, January.

DFID, 2011, *Social Science Research in India: A Mapping Report,* New Delhi: South Asia Research Hub.

Endu Palit Amit, 2009, "Skills Development in India: Challenges and Strategies". *ISAS Working Paper,* National University of Singapore, No. 89.

Gopal Ramamirtham, 2015, "The Great Funds Chase", *The Hindu*, Education Plus, 3rd August.

ICSSR, 2007, *Restructuring the Indian Council of Social Science Research*, (Report of the Fourth Review Committee) New Delhi: ICSSR.

International Commission on Peace and Food, 1989, *Developing Human Resourcefulness*, California: International Commission on Peace and Food.

Jeroen Huigman and Jan Currie, 2004, "Accountability in Higher Education: Bridge over Troubled Water?" *Higher Education* 48:4C, December.

Education Joseph Thomas, 2015, "Commission *Versus* Commission in Higher", *The Hindu*, 3rd August.

Kanagasabapathi, P., 2012, *Indian Models of Economy, Business and Management*, New Delhi: PHI Private Limited.

Keefer Philip, 2009, "The Poor Performance of Poor Democracies" in *The Oxford Handbook of Comparative Politics* (eds.) Carles Boix and Susan C. Stokes, New Delhi: Oxford University Press.

Leah Falca Vanita and Khamuja Jasmeet, 2015, "India's Unrealized Maternity Entitlements", *The Hindu*, 28th March.

Majaratna Arup. 2014, "Invasion of Educational Universes by Neo-Liberal Economic Thinking: A Civilization Casualty?" *Economic and Political Weekly*, XLIX: 37, 13th September.

Manor James, 2010, "*Local Governance*" in Niraja Gopal Jayal and Pratap Bhanu Metha (eds.) *The Oxford Companion Politics in India*, New Delhi: Oxford University Press.

Mjelde Liv and Daly Richard (eds.), 2009, *Working Knowledge in a Globalized World*, Berlin: Peter Lang.

Mathur, 2009, *Policy Research Organizations in South Asia*, New Delhi: IDRC.

Ministry of Human Resource Development, 2009, *Report of the Committee to Advice on Renovation and Rejuvenation of Higher Education*, New Delhi: Government of India.

Ministry of Labour and Employment, 2009, *National Policy on Skill Development 2009*, New Delhi: Government of India.

National Knowledge Commission *Report to the Nation 2006*, New Delhi: National Knowledge Commission, 2009.

Pawan Agarwal, 2007, "From Kothari Commission to Pitroda Commission", *Economic and Political Weekly*, 17th February.

Pawan Agarwal, 2009, *Indian Higher Education: Envisioning the Future*, New Delhi: Sage Publications.

Pandian, M.S.S., 2002, "Social Science in South India", *Economic and Political Weekly*, Vol. XXXVII, No. 5, 31st August.

Palanithurai, G., 2005, "Extension in Higher Education: The Missing Dimension", *University News*, Vol. 43, No. 17, June.

Palanithurai, G., 2013, "Are the Youth Liability or Asset?" *Puthiyathalaimurai Kalvi* (in Tamil), Vol. 3, No. 22, 14th January.

Palanithurai, G., 2006, "Larger Role of Academics in Rural Human Life", *University News*, Vol. 47, No. 16, April.

Palanithurai, G., 2009, "Rural Universities in the Era of Globalization", *University News*, Vol. 74, No. 33, August.

Palanithurai, G., 2007, *Globalization: Concerns at the Grassroots and How to Address them?*, Gandhigram: Rajiv Gandhi Chair for Panchayati Raj Studies.

Palanithurai, G., 2012, *Social Relevance of Higher Learning Institutions*, New Delhi: Concept Publishing Company Pvt. Ltd.

Palanithurai, G., 2015, *Students in the Field: An Experimental Learning Village Placement Programme*, New Delhi: Concept Publishing Company (P) Ltd., p. 65.

Palanithurai, G., 2008, *Ten Years of Experience in Decentralization Gandhigram*: Rajiv Gandhi Chair for Panchayati Raj Studies.

Palanithurai, G., 2007, *Vision of Rajiv Gandhi on Local Governance*, New Delhi: Concept Publishing Company Pvt. Ltd.

Palanithurai, G., 2009, "Larger Role of Academics in Rural Human Life", *University News*, Vol. 47, No. 16, April.

Palanithurai, G., 2009, "Rural Universities in the Era of Globalization", *University News*, Vol. 47, No. 33, August.

Palanithurai, G., 2009, *Empowering People through Empowering Panchayats: Experience in Ten Years in Panchayats*, Gandhigram: Rajiv Gandhi Chair for Panchayati Raj Studies.

Palanithurai, G., 2002, *Capacity Building Exercises for Local Body Leaders*, New Delhi: Concept Publishing Company (P) Ltd.

Pilz Mathias and Sarrah Pierenkemper Dipl. Kffr, 2014, "Apprenticeship Programmes—Lessons from Germany and German Companies in India", *The Indian Journal of Industrial Relations*, Vol. 49, No. 3, January.

Purnima Kishwar Madhu, 2005, *Deepening of Democracy: Challenges of Governance and Globalization in India*, New Delhi: Oxford University Press.

Panikkar, K.N., 2009, "Towards a New Paradigms in Education", *The Hindu*, 9th May.

Ramachandran, R., 2009, "University Business", *Frontline*, July 17.

Rajini Kothari, 2005, *Rethinking Democracy*, Hyderabad: Orient Longman.

Rajiv Gandhi Chair, 2007, *Ten Years of Experience in Decentralization*, Gandhigram: Rajiv Gandhi Chair for Panchayati Raj Studies.

Rajkumar, C., 2007, "Academic Freedom and Higher Education", *The Hindu*, 13th November.

Rhodes G. and Sporn B. (2002) "Quality Assurance in Europe and the US: Professional and Political, Economic Framing of Higher Education Policy 141' " *Higher Education*, 43 : 3.

Siva, Meera, 2014, "How to Train Your Population", *Business Line*, 5th August.

Shah, Mihir, 2015, *"Tribal Alienation in an Unequal India"*, *The Hindu*, 4th July.

Sohomi Milind, 2015, "The University and Development Agenda", *Economic and Political Weekly*, Vol. L: No.11, 14th March.

Sampat, Preeti, 2015, "Growth for a few and loss for many", *The Hindu*, 28th March.

Sharma, Ravi, 2009, "Main Markets", *Frontline* July, 17.

Salmi, J., 2000, *Tertiary Education in the 21st Century: Challenges and Opportunities*, Washington DC: World Bank.

Sanchita Bakshi *et al.*, 2015, "Regional Disparities in India: A moving frontier" *Economic and Political Weekly*, 3rd January.

Stella, Anthony and Gnanam, A., 2004, *Looking Ahead: A Decade of Accreditation in Retrospect: Development in Quality Assurance of Higher Education in India*, Bangalore, Aicra Publishers.

Thorat Sukhadeo, 2015, "A Blueprint for Higher Education", *The Hindu*, 11th August.

Thomas, Joseph, 2007, "Commission *versus* Commission in Higher Education", *Economic and Political Weekly*, December 15.

UGC, 2007, *A Brief Report of the National Conference on Development of Higher Education*, New Delhi: UGC.

UGC, 2009, *Report of the Commission to Advise on Renovation and Rejuvenation of Higher Education*, New Delhi: UGC.

Visvanathan, Shiv, 2015, "A New Public Policy for a New India: *The Hindu*, 6th April.

Viswanathan, S., 2009, "Tamil Nadu", *Frontline*, July, 17.

Viramani, A., 2002, "A New Development Paradigm: Employment, Entitlement and Empowerment", *Economic and Political Weekly*, Vol. 37, (22).

Reports from Gandhigram Rural Institute

Impact of MGNREGA – A Case Study Analysis, 2012, Gandhigram: Department of Political Science and Development Administration, Group I.

Participation of People in Panchayat, 2012, Gandhigram: Department of Political Science and Development Administration, Group II.

Women's Empowerment through SHGs, Gandhigram: Department of Political Science and Development Administration, 2012. Group III.

People's Participation in Gram Sabha, Gandhigram: Department of Political Science and Development Administration, 2012. Group IV.

Accountability in Gram Panchayat, Gandhigram: Department of Political Science and Development Administration, 2012. Group V.

Transparency in Functioning of Panchayat, Gandhigram: Department of Political Science and Development Administration, 2012. Group VI.

Service Delivery through Report Card, Gandhigram: Department of Political Science and Development Administration, 2012. Group VII.

Traditional Panchayats, Gandhigram: Department of Political Science and Development Administration, 2012. Group VIII.

Index